WINDSOR & ETON
Centuries of Change

WINDSOR & ETON
Centuries of Change

Sheila Rooney

Illustrations:

Pamela Marson

Daphne Fido

Museum Collection of the
Royal Borough of Windsor and Maidenhead

breedon **books**
PUBLISHING

First published in Great Britain in 2002 by
The Breedon Books Publishing Company Limited
Breedon House, 3 The Parker Centre,
Derby, DE21 4SZ.

Dedication
To my husband, Pat.
Patient listener, benevolent critic.

ISBN 1 85983 310 1

Printed and bound by Butler & Tanner, Frome, Somerset,
England.

Cover printed by Lawrence-Allen Colour Printers,
Weston-super-Mare, Somerset, England.

CONTENTS

ACKNOWLEDGEMENTS

The illustrations and information in this book have come from many sources and I am grateful to the chairman and members of the Windsor Local History Publications Group particularly, Beryl Hedges for permission to use her extensive collection of old postcards, Dr Judith Hunter for reading the text and making corrections, Jane Langton for her knowledge of church history, Dr Brigitta Mitchell for her knowledge of Windsor's military history, and Kathleen Whelan, Geoffrey Try, Joyce Sampson, Ellen Dollery, Margaret Gilson and Jean Kirkwood, for the loan of photographs and research material.

Many of the illustrations have come from the Museum Collection of the Royal Borough of Windsor and Maidenhead and I am grateful for permission to use the photographs in the collection and for the help of Heritage Officer, Olivia Gooden. While researching in the collection at Tinker's Lane, I was assisted by the Friends of the RBWMMC including Ron Hudson, Leslie Grout, Norman Oxley and Colin Hague.

Although I have tried to include everyone who has a part in the preparation of this book, if I have left anyone out I apologise. My thanks to the following:

The Mayor's Secretary, Betty Langhorne, and former Councillors David Drye, Peter Gray and Baroness Flather. The staff of the libraries of Windsor and Dedworth and the archivist of Eton College. Sylvia Wisbey, Clare Newton, Frank Bond, Frank Radnor, Joan Epps, Neville Wridgway, Richard Russell, Joyce Gillingham, Marcia Richardson and Harry Graves also loaned photographs.

Permission for the use of copies of their photographs was given by the editor of the *Windsor and Eton Express* [Press photographs of Windsor And Eton], English Heritage [Bedford Lemere photographs of St Leonard's Hill], The Guide Association [the Queen as a Sea Ranger], Leicestershire Record Office [G. Henton's photographs of Windsor and Eton], Sue Milton [photographs of the River Thames], Guildhall Art Gallery [photograph of the tapestry from the Windsor Tapestry].

My special thanks are due to Daphne Fido for her drawings and, most of all, to Pam Marson who provided most of the modern photographs in the book.

Saxon Footprints, Norman Masters

WINDSOR is dominated by its ancient castle, one of the largest fortresses in the world, which looms powerfully over the town and dominates the skyline. In the 10 centuries of its existence its image as a stronghold has rarely been challenged, but it serves effectively as a great symbol for the kingdom and the monarchy. From the earliest days of its existence the town, which grew up beside the castle, depended on the fort for safety and trade. The early Saxon villagers soon learned that its builder, William the Conqueror, was both harsh and ruthless.

After the defeat of the Saxon King Harold at Hastings, William of Normandy went on to conquer the rest of the country and, having ejected the Saxon lords from their manors, gave their lands to his Norman knights. Not surprisingly the hostile, defeated English had to be subdued and the new design of Norman castle was ideal for this task. Technically, it was the most advanced construction of the time, both for defending land which had been conquered and for subjugating a hostile population.

Construction began with the digging of a circular mound surrounded by a ditch. With Windsor the ditch remained a dry moat as the effort of bringing up water from the river would have taxed the power of the early builders. The mound or motte was crowned with a wooden keep (which was replaced with a stone tower a century later) and around it was an open area known as the bailey which provided protection for animals, men and stores. This also was protected by a mound and ditch, fortified with a wooden defence. Thus the plan of the castle was established early and remained much the same over the centuries.

England before the Norman Conquest was not a single country but a group of rival kingdoms. Constant changes of boundaries meant that Windsor belonged to different kingdoms at different times but it became part of Wessex in the ninth century, the most powerful of the kingdoms.

As we can see from the extract of the Domesday Book the names of the Saxon settlements around the castle still exist, although the modern spelling needs translation. Clivore, meaning 'the place of the cliff dwellers', is now Clewer and Dideorde is Dedworth. Windlesore, the old name for Windsor, is now Old Windsor and was an important Saxon site where there was a royal palace used by Edward the Confessor. During excavations of the site in 1951 quantities of Saxon pottery were unearthed and a small decorative metal dress ornament known as the 'Kingsbury Beast' was found. The archaeological finds at Old Windsor appeared to confirm that this was the remains of a Saxon manor house and most likely the residence of Edward the Confessor, with the nearby Windsor Forest serving as the royal hunting ground.

The land on which the castle was built belonged to Ralf, one of William's Norman knights. It had a high chalk bluff which was an ideal situation to build a fort as it was protected on one side by the river and had extensive views over the surrounding countryside. So William had to lease it back from Siegfried, the son of Ralf. As the castle developed, workers and traders were attracted to the new site which offered employment and a measure of safety. By the reign of Henry I the castle had become a royal residence with the king holding court there for the first time in 1110. After that Old Windsor declined while a new town developed outside the castle which was called New Windsor to distinguish it from the older settlement.

The River Thames was the main freight route into the interior and up it were brought building materials and supplies. Windsor was of exceptional military importance as it dominated the middle reaches of the Thames.

Windsor Castle was one of a ring of forts built by William to control the area round London and each was approximately a day's march away from its neighbour. Today only two of these castles remain habitable; the Tower of London and Windsor Castle. All the others have disappeared or are in ruins.

Across the water lay Eton, which was in existence long before Windsor. Its Saxon name meant 'a settlement on an island'. The fact that there was – and still are – lammas lands in the parish is proof that the Saxons had arrangements which allowed all householders to graze animals at certain periods. The manor of Eton (Ettone in Domesday) was held by Queen Edith, wife of Edward the Confessor, at the time of the Norman Conquest. Later records show that William FitzOther, Constable of Windsor Castle and another of William's followers, obtained the manor in the ensuing years.

Walter FitzOther's descendants were Constables of the castle and held the manor until 1204 when two sisters, daughters of Walter de Windsor, inherited the manor, as there were no male heirs.

The manor was split between them and the part inherited by Christina Lascelles was again divided when some of it was granted by Christina's son to King John's son, Richard. The main part of Christina's inheritance came into royal hands in the reign of Edward III. This may have been the manor that was granted to Eton College by Henry VI soon after its foundation. It was taken back in 1465 and remained in Crown hands until 1942 when Eton College bought it and, with the other part acquired in 1948, reunited almost all of Queen Edith's Saxon estate in Eton.

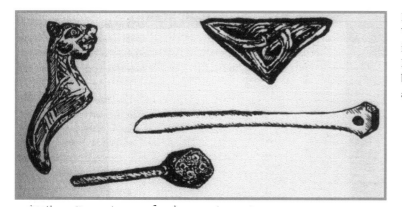

Finds from the Old Windsor excavations include the Kingsbury Beast, a triangular gilt-bronze plate, a bronze pin and a bone bodkin.

King Edward the Confessor as depicted on the Bayeux Tapestry. When Edward was a boy, much of England was dominated by the pagan Danes so he was sent away to Normandy to be brought up as a Christian hence the name Confessor. In many ways he was more Norman than Saxon as his mother was Emma of Normandy. His father was the Saxon king, Ethelred the Unready. Edward seems to have favoured Old Windsor because of the available hunting in Windsor Forest.

This section of the Bayeux Tapestry shows Edward the Confessor, with crown and sceptre, seated on a stool or backless throne. This image also appears on the surviving seals of the period.

The excavations at Old Windsor uncovered the remains of a timber structure which may have looked like this and could have been Edward the Confessor's 'palace'.

William the Conqueror ordered a survey of England to establish what was owed to him in taxes. The written record is known as the Domesday Book and includes entries for Clewer (Clivore), Dedworth (Dideorde), Windsor (Windesores) and Eton (Ettone). The initial part of Domesday was completed by 1087.

The font in St Andrew's Church, Clewer, is circular in shape and ornamented with eight panels of semi-circular arches enclosing an image of a bursting pea-pod.

The Old English word *windelsora* means 'river bank with a windlass'. A windlass was used to haul up cargo from a river boat.

The detail of a bursting pea-pod which may have some connection with Peascod Street.

On the Bayeux Tapestry William's men are shown building a motte, after the death of King Harold at Hastings. This type of fortification enabled William to successfully hold down his captured kingdom.

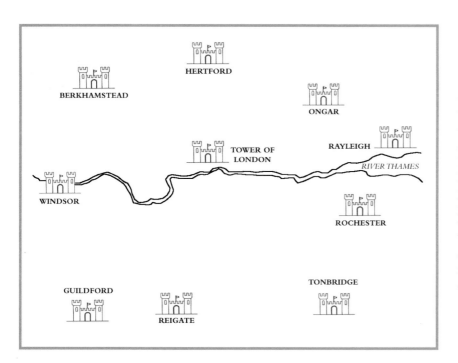

The Saxons were not castle builders and this was probably the main reason the Normans could keep them under control. In addition to the Tower of London, the centre of Norman power, William built a protective ring of castles. Each was about a day's match apart. With the exception of the Tower and Windsor Castle, nothing more than ruins remains of this defensive shield.

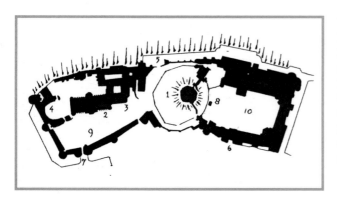

The basic plan of Windsor Castle has remained unchanged since the Middle Ages, although it has been continually developed. Key: 1. The Round Tower. 2. St George's Chapel. 3. Albert Memorial Chapel. 4. Horseshoe Cloisters. 5. North Terrace. 6. George IV Gateway. 7. Henry VIII Gateway. 8. Charles II Statue. 9. Lower Ward. 10. Upper Ward.

The Curfew Tower is on the west front of the Lower Ward and contains the earliest known remains of the original castle. The clock at the top of the tower was made by John Davis of Windsor (1653–1713).

A collection of relics were found on St Leonard's Hill in 1700 and amongst them was this bronze lamp which was presented to the Society of Antiquaries by William Stukely, an important member of the society. It was at first thought to be a Roman lamp but scholars in the 1950s confirmed that it belonged to the mediaeval period. It is now thought to have belonged to the original Hermitage.

Hermits were the holy men of the 11th and 12th centuries. They lived simply and devoted their lives to prayer. The hermit of St Leonard's, Clewer, was famous in the mediaeval period and the Church granted an indulgence to those pilgrims who visited the hermit, prayed with him and left alms for the church.

St Andrew's Parish
Church at Clewer is
the oldest building
in Windsor.
Although mostly
Norman it has a
Saxon font and
parts of the south
wall show a Saxon
influence.

Servicing Windsor Castle: The Guildhall, traders and the growth of trading

THE castle was the reason for the development of the town in the first place. It is probable that, even as the motte was being dug, enterprising farmers were selling provisions to the hungry Norman troops rather than have the goods stolen from them. As the fortress grew bigger and bigger, the castle clearly became of greater importance than the Old Windsor Palace, so a settlement of enterprising farmers, craftsmen and labourers no doubt gathered nearby, ready to trade, and comforted by the associated protection afforded by the fortress. In a period of weakened Saxon alliances, protection was probably a primary reason for the development of the town.

If we look at today's map we can still see the pattern of that early development in the area of small streets across from the castle. Their former names have echoes of their mediaeval function as Church Street was once Fish Street and Butcher's Row is now Market Street. This is where the first traders coming from Old Windsor set up their stalls. It has been suggested that there is an element of town planning, perhaps instigated by Henry I, in the way the area developed. Today there are two streets which still follow the mediaeval plan. One street, which is now Thames Street, High Street and Park Street all joined together, runs from Windsor Bridge to Cambridge Gate; forming a crossroads at its centre is Peascod Street, which runs westward towards the forest.

Markets and fairs were the most important ways of buying and selling and attracted people from a wide area. The right to hold a fair was granted by the king and taxes and tolls were payable for the permission to sell goods in the market or fair. From the demands of the market developed the need for trade control. This was the beginning of Windsor's merchant community. They had earned the right to trade, following years of apprenticeship and study, and were not going to allow others to invade their rights and profits without due payment.

Prosperous mediaeval towns all had markets and many towns still have their market cross, not necessarily in its original use as the centre of a functioning market, but more likely now as a decorative historic feature. Windsor's market cross stood on the central space which is now occupied by a statue of Queen Victoria. Although the cross appears in *Foxe's Book of Martyrs* (1563) Norden's map of 1607 does not show it. In 1592 a large new market house was built just to the north of the present Guildhall. The Guildhall was the civic centre for the town of Windsor and functioned as a town hall and market house.

The river was also a most important

highway for the transport of goods and the movement of people. Kings travelled to Windsor by barge from London. Stone for the castle came downstream from Oxford and upstream from Caen in Normandy. Timber was moved in great quantities and the wharfside by the bridge was effectively Windsor's front door, since from Saxon times it was known as the place where a windlass could lift goods from the riverboats on to the bank.

The granting of Windsor's Charter of Freedom on 28 May 1277 was, for the town, the starting point of its emergence from its dependence on the Crown. It meant that New Windsor became a free borough responsible for managing its own affairs. The borough then had the right to collect tolls and it was authorised to form a guild of merchants to undertake the supervision of commerce. The Corporation, although it did not use this name until the 15th century, took over the functions of the Merchant Guild and spent much of its time regulating the trade within the borough and safeguarding its own traders against 'foreigners', i.e. traders from anywhere outside Windsor. By 1683 this meant that only 'freemen' could carry on any retail trade within the borough. Admission to 'freeman' status was usually by the serving of an apprenticeship of seven years or by birth.

This function died out in the late 18th century and now the Freedom of the Borough exists as an honour bestowed on distinguished people such as the high steward.

Under the reigns of the mediaeval kings, including Edward II, Edward III and Richard II, several charters confirmed the terms of the original charter and the town continued to flourish until the catastrophic plagues of the Middle Ages which resulted in the depopulation of the town. In 1439 Henry VI granted a new charter giving the town financial help and increasing the power of civil and criminal jurisdiction over its inhabitants.

An inquiry in 1439 revealed that the town had become 'empty and wasted' and it was not until the Tudor era that some of the town's prosperity would return.

Throughout the Middle Ages, Old Windsor and Clewer were separate parishes. Their local government was in the hands of the lord of the manor who had power over the land and the tenants of his estate.

By 1520 prosperity had returned to Windsor. The castle was a favoured royal residence bringing nobles, courtiers and business to the town. New houses were being built to accommodate wealthy merchants and master craftsmen. Between 1653 and 1725 of 50 mayors, 13 were providers of food including cheesemongers, butchers, confectioners, bakers and grocers. Seven mayors were craftsmen including armourer, clockmaker, blacksmith, carpenter, glazier, goldsmith and a paint-strainer. Not surprisingly, as everyone drank beer, five mayors came from brewing or the provision of wine. The leading burgesses were thus men providing services to the castle, chapel and garrison and the people of the town. Only one mayor was a farmer and of the 326 men who were admitted as freemen only 19 were farmers or rivermen. Windsor, from being an agricultural community had changed into a mercantile and craft community.

The historic Windsor Bridge, that linked Windsor and Eton, was vital to the development of both towns, but in particular Windsor which relied upon it to bring supplies to the castle from the old road known as the King's Way to Sloo (Slough). It was the responsibility of Windsor to maintain the bridge and, in 1236, oak trees in the royal forest on the Great Park were felled for use in its repair. However, in 1277, there were concerns that the bridge was not fit for horses and carts to pass over it. A system of tolls was introduced to raise funds, which taxed all boats and cargoes passing under the bridge as well as people and goods travelling over it. This tax proved extremely unpopular, even more so because the funds were raised did not always go towards maintaining the bridge. In 1898, following a lengthy legal battle, the bridge was declared toll-free.

In the years before the college was built Eton was a thriving town and served the castle across the river. It had its own merchants and commerce all based on the site where the college now stands. The granting of a charter to hold a fair in Eton in 1238 was important to the townspeople, as was permission to hold a market that was granted to Roger de Caux at the same time.

In spite of its low-lying position – the nature of the river caused much flooding – Eton survived because barges were the most efficient way of moving bulky goods and the river was a principal highway. As the vessels moved up and down the Thames, Eton became a useful supplier of refreshment and succour for the rivermen. There were plenty of alehouses and places to eat, serving the eels and fish which were so plentiful. Along the bank grew osiers which were made into baskets, the main containers for goods and produce.

The river also provided a power source to drive the mills, of which Eton seems to have had two.

The Elizabethan Market House had an open area in the lower part which served as a Corn Market. In the background, shown in this photograph of a diorama of Tudor Windsor, is the old parish church. By the late 17th century the Market House was described as 'ruinous and ready to fall down' so the council ordered it to be pulled down and by 1690 it had been replaced by the present Guildhall.

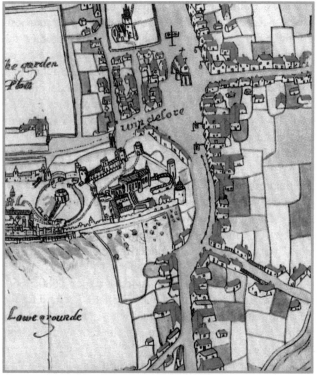

In William Collier's map of Windsor, 1742, the street pattern had changed little since Norden's map of 1607.

Norden's map shows the Elizabethan Market House which was built in 1592. Near the Guildhall can be seen the town whipping post and pillory. At the junction of Castle Street and the High Street there stood the mediaeval market cross which Norden has not included on his map.

The civic heart of New Windsor was the Guildhall which has stood on its present site for nearly 300 years. The present building was built 1687–90 and extended in 1829. Beneath the extension was an open area where meat and poultry was sold and the corn exchange also took place. The Guildhall served as town hall and was where the town council met. It also housed the courts of justice and administration. Balls and concerts took place there along with banquets and other social events.

This building, which features in many a tourist's photographs, was once a butcher's shop owned by Silas Bradbury. An older building had been purchased by his great-grandfather in 1656 for £82 as a shop and dwelling house. The area around it had been used by the town butchers and was known as 'the Shambles'. In 1718 Silas demolished the old building and set about rebuilding his shop, only to find himself in dispute with the mayor, Thomas Rutter, and the Corporation. It was claimed that the land on which he was digging his foundations belonged to the Corporation. An expensive legal action followed which found in Silas Bradbury's favour. Silas built his new shop and dwelling house in the early 18th century. The timber-framed building now leans precariously to the north, apparently the result of building too tall a house on that site. Its present name is a fairly modern one as it never was the Market Cross or the Market House.

A plaque on a wall in Queen Charlotte Street informs us that this is the shortest street in the country.

The mediaeval pattern of cobbled streets at the gates of the castle exists today, although their old names have been superseded by new ones. Fish Street, which dates from the time when it served as a fish market, is now St Alban's Street. Behind many of the façades of the shops can be found the old timber-framed buildings.

Church Street.

Market Street.

Church Lane.

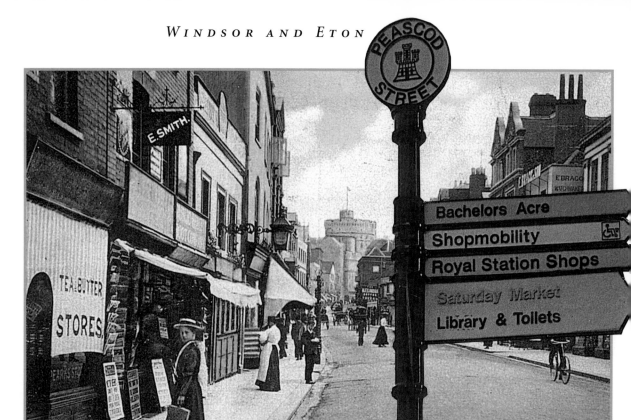

Peascod Street is probably the oldest street in town. The road follows a natural watershed and was a routeway between forest, castle and river crossing. The name derives from a croft where peas were grown.

Christopher Wren was one of England's most famous architects. He was born in 1632 in East Knoyle, Wiltshire, but in his early years his father became Dean of Windsor so the family lived in the Deanery within the walls of Windsor Castle. He first made his mark as a Professor of Astronomy at London's Gresham College in 1657 and became Surveyor General to Charles II. The building of Windsor's Guildhall was supervised by him and by 1672 he had been knighted by the king.

Sir Christopher's house in Thames Street, which is now a hotel, was built in 1672. Records show that in 1788 it was lived in by the Jervoise family who wanted to be near their son who was at Eton College. Later the house was owned by a bargemaster and coal merchant who built extra stables and opened a gateway that led to a wharf.

The bridge, seen here from the Windsor side, has for centuries been a busy thoroughfare for people and vehicles passing between Windsor and Eton. Eventually the heavy burden of motor traffic became too much for it and it was closed to traffic and pedestrianised.

This picture of the diorama, which shows Windsor Bridge in the 18th century, has the figure of the artist Paul Sandby sketching on the right-hand side. The earliest bridge was probably constructed in the 13th century and has been the main link between Windsor and Eton throughout the centuries.

In 1898, after a legal battle lasting three years that was led by Joseph Taylor, the case concerning the payment of tolls for using the bridge reached the House of Lords. The Lords judged that Windsor Bridge should be free of tolls.

The High Street, or Altus Vicus as it was called in the earliest surviving lease of 1398, has long been the main street of the town. From earliest times the street was the centre of Windsor's busy market.

A Tesco supermarket arrived in Dedworth in 1994 and had a devastating effect on the parades of small shops which served the area.

This parade of shops in a modern housing area was one of the casualties following the arrival of the Tesco supermarket.

William Herbert's department store was packed with thousands of items in its 24 departments and was claimed to be 'the largest and best equipped store outside London'. Like Harrods in Knightsbridge, virtually any item could be supplied to order. The store held the Royal Warrant, not only of Queen Victoria but also of 12 other European royals. Prior to World War One, Herbert's games department stocked every imaginable game available. William Herbert died in 1906, and in 1924–5 the store ceased trading. For some years the premises were used by Cullin's Garage before demolition in 1980.

The changing face of Daniel's which evolved from humble haberdashers in Peascod Street to the refurbished departmental store with entrances in King Edward Court and Peascod Street.

The ticket office and other buildings were part of the Windsor and Eton Central Railway Station. The station was rebuilt and enlarged by the Great Western Railway Company in 1897, as part of Queen Victoria's Diamond Jubilee celebrations. In 1979 work began on the 'Royalty and Empire' Exhibition staged by Madame Tussauds. In 1991 the station was bought from Madame Tussauds by property developers (AXA) who converted it into a retail area which opened in 1997 and includes many of the famous high street names.

The entrance from King Edward Court to the shopping area of Windsor Royal Station.

The restaurant known as The Cockpit which is 47-49 High Street, Eton, dates back to at least 1420 according to deeds which refer to the property being sold by the deans and canons of St George's Chapel to John Strugnell. The Strugnell descendants owned the property for several centuries. The name comes from the use of the cobbled yard at the rear of number 49, which was the scene of countless cockfights in the 17th and 18th centuries. The old knucklebone floor had a useful a non-slip surface which helped the fighting cocks keep their balance.

Originally the building consisted of three cottages and, in the early part of the 20th century, the end cottage was lived in by a cobbler whose neighbours were two elderly ladies. In 1928 a Mrs Rigden bought the cottages and adapted them into an antique shop where she also served teas. Later a grocer's shop was included. The stocks were thought to have come from Clewer and placed in front of the shop in the 1930s. In 1971 the property was bought by Janet and Vittoria Bianchi and converted into the fine restaurant it is today.

Situated beside the Cockpit restaurant, the post box is in the 1856 style.

This set of stocks which stand outside the Cockpit are believed to have come from Clewer. They were a common means of punishment for centuries. The wrongdoer was placed in a sitting position in the timber frame with the ankles confined between the planks of wood.

The idea behind the Royal Warrant Holder is as old as the monarchy itself. Someone had to supply the monarch with his robes and food and fix the roof of the castle. There were, of course, trading benefits to such patronage. Today there are 850 Royal Warrant Holders who are allowed to display the Royal Arms with the words 'By Appointment' and include big public companies as well as tiny shops.

The Windsor, Eton and District Royal Warrant Holders Association number about 60 members and include the castle chimney sweep and Sandersons, the wallpaper manufacturer. Douglas Hill (left) is the secretary of the Windsor and Eton Warrant Holders Association. His Eton High Street shop is also an off-licence where he sells the wines of his native New Zealand. Now he does the royal family's prescriptions, a highly personal service, for which those members of the royal family above pensionable age pay no charge. He also supplies prescriptions for the boys of Eton College.

In March 1840, the adult male parishioners attended a meeting in the Crown and Cushion to vote for the 'Vestrey', an elected body of Eton townspeople who ran the parish affairs. Later the 'Vestrey' would hold meetings in a room provided by the college.

After the college, the Christopher Inn is the institution with the longest history. It is mentioned as early as 1511 and was rebuilt in 1709. It removed from the old site in 1846.

The Waterman's Arms, Eton. In 1793 the building where The Waterman's Arms now stands was purchased by the parish of Eton to serve as a workhouse for the poor.

Eton High Street *c.*1800.

Soldier, Soldier: Regimental ceremony, State visits and the Order of the Garter

THE soldiers in Windsor are such a fixture in the town scene that we tend to forget the reasons for the establishment of the garrison. The soldiers have always been in Windsor ever since the castle was under construction when those first Norman knights and their followers commandeered the land, evicted the Saxon landowners and erected their motte and bailey fort, which also served as a prison for defeated but defiant victims.

Windsor without soldiers would be like an opera without the chorus. The backdrop is there in the shape of the majestic castle and the royal family take the leading roles. The audience is there too, filled with townsfolk and swelled by tourists. Take away the soldiers and the orchestra, and the pageantry would disappear. Nearly every day the soldiers march up the High Street and pass the Guildhall with their drums beating and their bands playing on the way to the castle for the Changing of the Guard, further dramatised by the stamp of boots and the shouts of command. An official visit by a head of state gives an enhanced free spectacle of regimental show and splendour.

The garrison is there because the castle is a fort and throughout history the size of the garrison has depended on the need for the monarchy to be protected. Although the monarch is no longer in permanent residence at Windsor, and our present Queen moves regularly to her other castles and houses, throughout history there have been periods when the monarch has been elsewhere, travelling around the kingdom. The castle has been under siege twice but it has never been vanquished.

One of the first sieges was in 1193 when King Richard was on a crusade and his brother John attempted to seize the crown. He appears to have been in possession of the castle, a situation which was resented by knights loyal to Richard who then besieged the castle for two months.

When John did succeed to the throne after the death of his brother, Richard, during a period of civil unrest in England, he chose Windsor for his refuge. John had been forced by his barons to seal Magna Carta, but he reneged on his promises to the barons and they asked the French king for help. Thus the second siege of Windsor Castle was by French knights in 1216. The Constable of the castle, Engelard de Cygony, with 60 knights and many foot soldiers, stoutly defended the castle for three months until the attacking force gave up and went away.

From early records we get some idea of

The pomp and ceremony of the annual Garter procession is a major part of Windsor's social calendar. People from all over the world, besides the town's residents, apply for tickets to watch the parade of Knights of the Garter, from the lawns surrounding St George's Chapel. The ceremony begins when the knights, wearing their distinctive mantles, assemble inside the state entrance to the chapel, while the military knights and officers of arms gather in the quadrangle, to await the Queen and the Duke of Edinburgh.

the military defence of the castle. In 1212 the bailiff and faithful men of Windsor were ordered 'to furnish 10 men and horses and arms, to be ready to serve the king when and where required'.

In 1242 we learn that Bernard de Savoy was paid £25 15s 0d monthly 'for the use of four knights, 11 soldiers and seven watchers, also a carpenter and some crossbow men'.

But the castle had no regular army in the modern sense until the 17th century when the country was divided by the Civil War. Ironically, the first garrison of any size in Windsor's royal castle was the anti-royalist Parliamentary army which was defying King Charles I. The town of Windsor itself had a strong Puritan element and so the area became a stronghold of Cromwell's supporters.

A fortress such as Windsor Castle should have been garrisoned with the king's soldiers but Charles had no standing army at his disposal. Parliament and the king realised the importance of Windsor, both for its strength and its commanding view of the countryside around it. In October 1642, the castle was attacked by the Royalist Prince Rupert whose five pieces of ordnance, firing from the grounds of Eton College, did considerable damage in the town, but the walls of the castle suffered very little damage.

The Civil War cast a long shadow over the town itself, as it became, for a period, the headquarters of the Parliamentary forces, with thousands of soldiers camping in the town. Although records show that the townspeople were sympathetic to the Parliamentary cause, nevertheless, the presence of the army must have strained their goodwill. Billeting laid on them an unbearable burden, particularly, for the numerous inns that had to supply most of the accommodation.

One letter, dating from this period, complains that 'all last winter we were charged with the billeting of soldiers, both horse and foot, to our exceeding hindrance and loss'.

Windsor had a small population living in houses which were often overcrowded even before the addition of soldiers. House-holders were often required to provide food and lodging for a certain number of men at a fixed rate, the payment for which was often deferred. There were artificial shortages of food and the price of basic commodities such as bread rose.

During the summer of 1643 pestilence was widespread and these conditions were bound to have strained relations between the townspeople and the soldiery.

Authority in the park and forest had broken down and, under these circum-stances, the poaching in the forest, accompanied by violence, resulted in the wholesale theft of the venison. In 1644 the soldiers under the command of the Parlia-mentarian, Lord Essex, slaughtered the deer so excessively that by the end of the war all the deer in the Great Park were wiped out.

In 1645 Windsor witnessed the mustering of the New Model Army which was to bring defeat to the king. Fairfax was appointed commander-in-chief and came to Windsor in the April of that year, as the Army was ready to march out. In its four weeks at

Windsor when the numbers in the army were more than 10 times the population of the town, the men must have either bivouacked or were quartered in the villages.

In June, after the Battle of Naseby, the Royalist army was shattered and nearly 5,000 prisoners, and all the king's artillery and baggage, fell into the hands of the victors.

Windsor remained a military centre to which disbanded soldiers returned for payment or more work, but eventually the money ran out and the men went hungry. Near the end of the fighting in July 1648 the castle was 'full of want and full of danger'.

The captured King Charles was brought to the castle and as he passed through the town, some of his people welcomed him and he was briefly happy to be back in Windsor. But on 19 January 1649, Charles I was transferred to London, where he was tried at Westminster Hall and later executed in Whitehall on 30 January, 1649. His body was returned to Windsor Castle and on 9 February, in a sombre procession to St George's Chapel, was interred in a vault.

Ten years of the Commonwealth, with its deeply unpopular military and religious dictatorship, was followed in 1658 by the death of Oliver Cromwell and the republic two years later. The monarchy was restored in 1660 and Windsor Castle once again became a royal residence.

Although the New Model Army had gone a large military presence continued with 300 soldiers quartered in the inns and houses. Soldiers became as they remain today, an important if shifting element in the life of the borough.

The routine of the garrison in earlier times is not well recorded but by 1660 the daily mounting guard had been established, a ceremony continued ever since.

A report of 1730, in the reign of George II, states. 'The number of soldiers allowed to do duty in this garrison is 40 men, 2 sergeants, 2 corporals, 2 drummers and a subaltern officer of the foot guards, who are relieved every 28 days by the like number.'

There was a notable change when the Duke of Montagu became Constable of the castle in 1781 and issued 'General Orders' which included the following:

'The sentries at the Round Tower, King's and Town Gates, are to keep everything quiet about their respective posts. No beggars or disorderly persons are upon any account to be allowed to stand in any of the gateways... No Higglers to be allowed to bring any meat, fish or greens to sell in the courtyard of the palace, nor are articles to be cried out for sale in any part of the palace.'

This suggests a tightening up of previously lax discipline which would undermine a military establishment responsible for the safety of the monarch. In the 1780s there was report of a riot at Windsor between a regiment of militia (Lancashire Volunteers) quartered there and the townsmen which was terminated by the interposition of cavalry.

By the time George III took up residence, little use was made of the castle's accommodation, which had suffered years of neglect. In addition, little of the pageantry associated with the monarchy remained in Windsor. Since the king had become more 'accessible', the public devotion to the notion of monarchy had increased, but Prime Minster William Pitt was still fearful of a British version of the French Revolution. Pitt was concerned that, in such an event, the military might well side with the people. To guard against this, Pitt segregated troops from the civilian population by the

construction of a barracks. Between 1795 and 1803, accommodation for 1,000 infantrymen was built in Sheet Street. Cavalry barracks, completed in 1804, were first occupied by the Blues.

One reason why the castle has been in constant use since the Middle Ages is the ceremony associated with the Most Noble Order of the Garter. This ancient order of Christian chivalry dates back to the reign of Edward III, who first established the order in 1344. After the Battle of Crecy in 1346, which followed Edward's claim to the kingdom of France, Edward III inaugurated

The Queen and the Knights of the Order of the Garter walk in procession from the Upper Ward to the chapel. On Monday 18 June 2001, two new knights were installed as Companions to the Most Noble Order of the Garter. In the above picture, the Princess Royal with the Prince of Wales and the Dukes of Kent and Gloucester are preceded by Garter Knights including Baroness Thatcher.

Near the door are the gentlemen at arms (personal bodyguard of the sovereign) below them are the Household Cavalry. The Garter Knights line the steps and the wives of the knights stand on the steps. Two cars arrive to take away the knights (the royal carriage has already left). The military knights are in a broken semi-circle and the Yeoman of the Guard line up on the lawn.

a different order of knighthood in Windsor. The new order would consist of only 26 young warriors who were the military companions of the king and his son, the Black Prince. Their motto *honi soit que mal y pense* meant 'evil he who that evil thinks' and St George was chosen as their patron saint.

The new Order of the Garter Knights sat in their special chapel in two groups, the king's knights on one side of the chapel and the prince's knights facing them on the other. Above the stalls in the chapel were hung the banners of the knights. There have been periods when the ceremony of instal-ling new knights has been exceptionally lavish, as in the reign of Henry VIII, and other times when it has hardly been celebrated. Knights are now drawn from leading statesmen as well as foreign monarchs. In this present reign, the ceremony of installing new knights is a colourful parade which takes place in June. Although today the ceremony is confined to the castle precincts, the lawns are packed with people to watch the royal family and the knights, which include all those newly installed as they walk down the Lower Ward towards the main entrance of St George's Chapel.

The 15th-century choir stalls are surmounted by the crests and banners of the members of the Order of the Garter.

A visit by a head of state is more likely to take place in Windsor nowadays because it is less disruptive to everyday life than those which centre on London and Buckingham Palace. Windsor Castle is an impressive backdrop to such a visit and troops of cavalry are a familiar sight in the town. This troop of Blues and Royals are part of the ceremonial parade for the visit of President Mbeki of South Africa.

A visit by a head of state usually includes an impressive show of regimental pageantry. The roads are sanded before the cavalry rides by to prevent the horses slipping.

Victoria Barracks. The building of barracks to house a regiment of infantry soldiers dates back to 1798. A Victorian extension was built between 1865–7, part of which can be seen in the illustration and which includes the officer's mess. This building was demolished and a modern building for the infantry was erected in the 1980s.

This is the original Combermere Barracks which accommodated one Cavalry regiment. On the left is K Block which housed the soldiers above the stables. After a visit by Queen Victoria in 1868, who was appalled at the conditions in which the soldiers lived, the stables were removed and verandas added to the building. Combermere Barracks were completely rebuilt in the 1960s.

This illustration of the diorama in the Royal Borough Museum Collection shows the castle at the time of the siege of the barons in 1216. Only the upper and middle baileys were built of masonry, the lower bailey was protected by earthworks and palisades.

This illustration is based on a painting by the artist Sandby who painted the scene in 1768 and shows the view through the Town Gate, looking westwards. The gate was adjacent to, but at right angles to, the Henry VIII Gateway and was built in the reign of Elizabeth I. There were a number of houses on Castle Hill above the Gateway which were demolished in the 19th century. The same fate befell the wall. We can see the hanging inn signs and the beer barrels which are being rolled towards them. The foot soldier may have been stationed in the castle.

A mounted officer of the Blues and Royals.

The funeral procession of Edward VII.

The funeral procession of George V.

This picture shows a few remaining Life Guards outside the garrison church. Every Sunday sightseers gathered outside the church in Claremont Road to see the colourful parade of the soldiers.

RELIGIOUS BUILDINGS: PERPENDICULAR GOTHIC, VICTORIAN AND SIMPLE MODERN

THE early churches in Windsor can be traced back to the time before William the Conqueror when Saxon churches existed both in Clewer and Old Windsor. Edward the Confessor worshipped in Old Windsor, but it is thought that William attended Mass in a wooden structure, possibly near what are now playing fields beside Imperial Drive.

In pre-Reformation days the Church was powerful and many churchmen held high office under the Crown. Its hierarchy was composed of its own great lords, arch-bishops and bishops, combining spiritual authority with administrative, political and economic power; below them came lesser bishops and abbots, who were influential in their own areas; and, finally, the parish clergy.

The early mediaeval period was one of great piety. Plague and famine stalked the population so it is no surprise that minds were on the hereafter, as death was always so close and could take its victims at any time. People had faith in their saints, and the relics of saints were believed to be of miraculous power. Any place of worship which held a holy relic became a place of pilgrimage. King Henry VI took pains to purchase relics for his new college at Eton because he knew that pilgrims would come to see them. It is often forgotten how frequently and how far mediaeval people travelled on pilgrimages. Such devotion was not discouraged by the

Church as pilgrims gave donations to the shrine or church, thus ensuring that it was kept in good repair. Many pilgrims visited the hermit on St Leonard's Hill and gave donations to the Hermitage.

The 12th and 13th centuries saw a growth in the power of the papacy, which led to clashes between the Pope and secular leaders over their respective spheres of jurisdiction. It is impossible to understand the social tensions of this period without mentioning the church at every point. At the very centre of power there were often clerical ministers governing the kingdom.

England came late to the Reformation which convulsed Europe. Henry VIII had been proclaimed by Pope Leo X, 'Defender of the Faith', a title still engraved on our coins. His first queen was the devout Catherine of Aragon and after their marriage the entire court moved to Windsor, bringing crowds of nobles and courtiers to the town. The Garter Ceremonies were particularly lavish with their spectacular cavalcades passing through the streets of Windsor and Eton.

Windsor played a major part in the drama of the king's matrimonial problems. Henry first saw Anne Boleyn when she sat sewing at the window in the Canon's Cloisters at Windsor Castle. It was at Windsor that he decided to set aside Catherine and marry Anne. After the beheading of Anne for treason, the king married his third wife, Jane Seymour, who, much to Henry's grief, died soon after the birth of his only son. Henry could not bear to attend her funeral and it was his daughter, Princess Mary, who took his place as chief mourner. Henry married three further wives before his death in January 1547, but it was his wish that he should be interred in the crypt of St George's Chapel beside the body of his beloved Jane Seymour.

During Henry's reign, many people were executed for their religious beliefs. These included three men named Filmer, Testwood and Pierson who were also known as 'The Windsor Martyrs'.

When Henry's daughter, Mary, ascended the throne in 1553, she reinstated the Mass

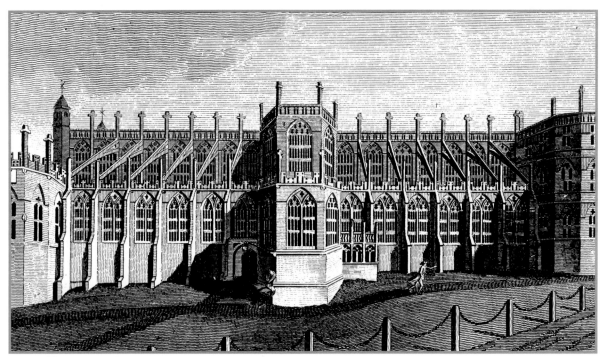

St George's Chapel is one of the most magnificent specimens of ecclesiastical architecture in the country; indeed, although technically only a chapel, local people in the 18th and early 19th centuries used to refer to it as 'the Cathedral'. In 1348, when Edward III founded the Most Noble Order of the Garter he restored the 13th-century chapel. It became the Order's chapel and was rededicated to Our Lady, St Edward and St George.

In the aftermath of the Wars of the Roses, the victorious Yorkist king, Edward IV, decided to build a new and much grander chapel. Across the Thames, his Lancastrian predecessor, Henry VI, had begun the chapel of his college at Eton in 1448. One can imagine the feelings of Edward IV as he viewed the fine new chapel at Eton, putting to shame the small chapel within the castle.

In 1475, Edward allowed the old great hall and vicar's lodgings to be swept away and work started on the new St George's. By the time Edward died in 1483, the great choir was finished, covered by a temporary wooden roof. Then in 1485, work on the chapel was suspended but later resumed, rather slowly, with several changes to design. The magnificent new window at the western end was added and the finest mason of his day, William Vertue, was put in charge of the work.

The result is a splendid example of Perpendicular Gothic architecture. St George's is one of the last great examples of the style. Light floods through the huge windows and the whole interior is richly magnificent.

During the Civil War, Commonwealth troops desecrated it and plundered its treasures but during the Restoration efforts were made to repair the damage. In the following centuries, several famous architects including Henry Emlyn and Sir Gilbert Scott left their mark on the chapel.

After the death of Albert, the Prince Consort, Queen Victoria ordered the complete restoration of the former Lady Chapel as a memorial to her beloved husband. The elaborate decoration of the Albert Memorial Chapel is a superb example of the craftsmanship of the Victorians.

With its Saxon origins, St Andrew's claims to be, not only the oldest church in Windsor but also the oldest building. Long before William the Conqueror started building his castle, there existed the riverside settlement and probably a wooden church on the site of the present building. It is built in the Norman style from chalk quarried nearby. The baptismal font, which may be all that remains of the earlier Saxon church, has an unusual decorative motif of pea pods running round the top border. Tradition has it that William attended mass in the small wooden church in Clewer, although there is also a suggestion that he had mass said by his chaplain in his lodge sited somewhere near Imperial Road.

and the Catholic practices of an earlier period. It was a time of calm and domestic improvement for St George's Chapel and the Poor Knights benefited from her generosity when new accommodation was provided for them.

During the period of the English Civil War, Windsor was largely a Puritan town, though one with a Royalist castle which was taken over by the Parliamentarians and controlled, on their behalf, by Fairfax. Even after the execution of Charles I and the establishment of the republican Commonwealth, a residue of both Dissenters and Anglicans remained.

After the Restoration, in 1676 during the reign of Charles II, there were some 115 known dissenters in an adult population of 1,025.

Many of these were Quakers, although the Congregationalists were the earliest of Windsor's Dissenting communities. In 1783, Methodist founder John Wesley wrote in his journal for 29 September: 'I declared the Gospel of Peace to a small company in Windsor'.

A population of Roman Catholics also lived in the area. At the beginning of the 18th century, Father John Chapman Vere St Leger, a Jesuit, was living at Spital and in 1727 a Portuguese priest, living under the name of Samuel Goltier, died in Windsor. Mass was still being celebrated in private houses for, although the fierce restrictions against

The original Church of St John the Baptist is early 12th century and even on Norden's map of 1607 it is drawn with a buttress supporting the tower. In the 17th and 18th centuries there are many records of repairs. In 1793 the *Windsor Guide* says that the interior was so designed that its system of large pews 'excluded the majority from attending Divine Service'. By the 1840s the work of the parish was left to the curate as the vicar lived elsewhere. In 1818 the church was in such a dilapidated state that it was resolved to build a new church which would 'fitly house the Established religion'. Between 1820–2 it was demolished and a new building designed by C. Hollis with Jeffry Wyattville, acting as advisor, replaced it.

Catholic worship had been lifted, there still remained enormous prejudice against Catholics and it was wiser for them to keep their faith hidden.

At the beginning of the 19th century the Church of England was still not flourishing. Anglicans had only two buildings, St John the Baptist which was the parish church of Windsor, and St Andrew's at Clewer. By 1900, however, there was a multiplicity of churches and chapels, both Anglican and others, buttressed by a system of church schools which at the start of the 21st century remains significant.

An illustration of the old Church of St John the Baptist before it was rebuilt in the 19th century. Two 17th-century monuments from the old church were retained as were the beautiful railings made by Grinling Gibbons in 1682 (originally from the private chapel in the castle) which now adorn the south chapel. A painting of the Last Supper by Frances de Cleyn is one of the church treasures.

The interior of St John The Baptist parish church.

An 18th-century view of Eton College Chapel from Windsor riverbank. In 1422, following the death of Henry V, his infant son, Henry VI, inherited the crown and it was this monarch who was to found the world famous school, Eton College. When Henry reached the age of 18 he obtained permission from the Pope to found the college of the Blessed Virgin Mary at Eton where there already existed a church dedicated to the Assumption of the Virgin. In the mediaeval period a college was a religious institution rather than an educational one and King Henry's foundation was to have a provost and fellows, priests and chaplains, singing men and bedesmen and a number of poor scholars.

In founding the college, Henry took over the parish church which was eventually demolished. His original plans for the chapel would have resulted in a building the size of a cathedral. However, during one of the king's bouts of insanity, Wayneflete (then Bishop of Winchester) took over the building of the chapel. The result was a more modest but still impressive building that we know today as Eton College Chapel.

Henry had purchased for the college some relics of the saints, which supposedly included a nail from the True Cross.

During the Wars of the Roses the battles between the Yorkists and the Lancastrian families caused dismay at Eton. Their fears were well-founded for when the Yorkist King Edward seized the crown he also removed some of the treasures from Eton, including their jewelled relics, vestments and furniture and deposited them within St George's Chapel.

The church of St Peter & St Andrew, Old Windsor, before renovations. There are suggestions that the site of the parish church of St Peter and St Andrew in Old Windsor is of very ancient religious significance with a hint that it may have Druid connections. What is known is that it was chosen for the consecration of Ethelsige as Abbot of St Augustine's in 1061. In 1070 the church was the setting for the Synod of Whitsuntide when Saxon prelates were replaced by Normans.

The date of 1216 is a sad one in the history of the church for that is the period when the French knights, who were the allies of King John, besieged Windsor Castle. Although they failed to seize the castle they damaged the church to such an extent that it had to be rebuilt in 1218.

In 1862, Sir Gilbert Scott was commissioned to renovate the church which he did in his characteristically thorough manner. The church was refaced with flint, its roof replaced, and out went the interior furnishings together with a large tomb and the church porch. Thus, the present church has 13th-century walls and windows and a 19th-century ceiling with late 19th-century interior.

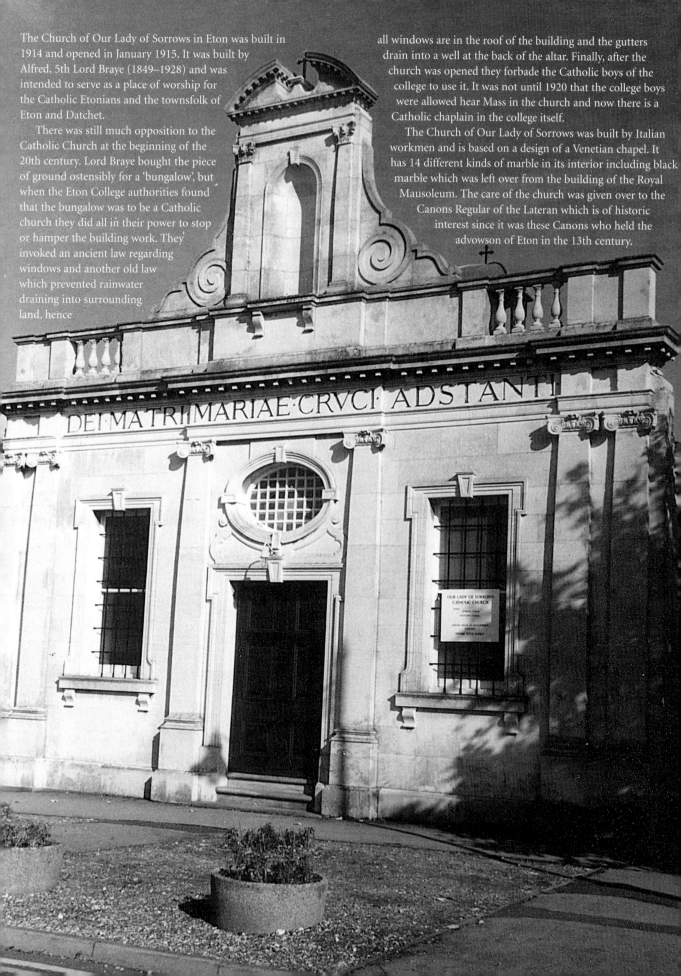

The Church of Our Lady of Sorrows in Eton was built in 1914 and opened in January 1915. It was built by Alfred, 5th Lord Braye (1849–1928) and was intended to serve as a place of worship for the Catholic Etonians and the townsfolk of Eton and Datchet.

There was still much opposition to the Catholic Church at the beginning of the 20th century. Lord Braye bought the piece of ground ostensibly for a 'bungalow', but when the Eton College authorities found that the bungalow was to be a Catholic church they did all in their power to stop or hamper the building work. They invoked an ancient law regarding windows and another old law which prevented rainwater draining into surrounding land, hence all windows are in the roof of the building and the gutters drain into a well at the back of the altar. Finally, after the church was opened they forbade the Catholic boys of the college to use it. It was not until 1920 that the college boys were allowed hear Mass in the church and now there is a Catholic chaplain in the college itself.

The Church of Our Lady of Sorrows was built by Italian workmen and is based on a design of a Venetian chapel. It has 14 different kinds of marble in its interior including black marble which was left over from the building of the Royal Mausoleum. The care of the church was given over to the Canons Regular of the Lateran which is of historic interest since it was these Canons who held the advowson of Eton in the 13th century.

St Mark's RC Church, Dedworth.

The Gospel Hall is the most recent building which can be classed as a place of worship. It is situated in Dedworth Road and is the meeting house of the Plymouth Brethren.

The beginnings of the Congregational Church in Windsor date from 1662 when after the restoration of Charles II an Act of Uniformity was passed by Parliament. This compelled every clergyman to take an oath of canonical obedience and those that refused i.e. dissenters, were ejected from their churches and homes. During the late 18th century small groups of people in Windsor met together to pray and there seems to have been such a group, meeting in Bier Lane. In 1804, the Revd Alexander Redford, became their first minister. A school was established and as their congregations expanded the church members decided to buy the site of the former theatre in High Street where they built the new 'Chapel of Dissenters'. This served as a place of worship until 1833 when the architect, Jessie Hollis, designed a new large church in William Street. In 1979 the foundation stone of the new Christ Church United Reformed was laid on the site of the demolished Congregational Church.

EDUCATION: FROM ANCIENT COLLEGE TO MODERN SCHOOLS

TEACHING and education was part of the Christian mission and were in the hands of the Church fathers. Pupils were of all ages and were taught by priests who were supervised by bishops. Thus the foundation of the educational system was controlled by the Church and it was not until the late 19th century that the State began to take an active part in the education of children.

In the Middle Ages the future prospects of the pupil was governed by their education. Boys educated in monasteries learned to read and write Latin, the language used by the Church, and most were destined to become priests or monks themselves.

In 1348, Edward III founded and endowed a college of canons to serve the St George's Chapel in Windsor Castle. There were 24 chaplains, some other ministers, and a dean who would be head of the college. There was also a song-school with six choristers who were paid to sing at the many ceremonial occasions connected with the Garter ceremony and at the king's wish. The boys would have been local children, perhaps the sons of the people living and working within the castle. St George's School is the earliest educational foundation in Windsor.

The fame of Eton College, which is known all over the world, has tended to overshadow the educational history of Windsor. Since the foundation of its charter in 1441 by Henry VI, Eton College has benefited from its proximity to Windsor Castle and from the patronage of many famous men who have been educated within its walls. Many British political leaders, as well as the sons of the aristocracy, have been educated there.

The royal founder of the college ordained 'that the college should maintain "public and general grammar schools", and, to enhance its position, forbade the establishment of similar schools at Windsor or elsewhere within ten miles of Eton'.

Eton did act as a grammar school in Windsor at least until the early part of the 19th century, but it is worth remembering that the school as Henry VI conceived was not only to consist of 70 poor scholars but also the sons of nobility and gentry who should attend as well as other boys, who paid for their own support and resided both in the college precincts and in the town.

In his *Eton College Register* 1698–1752, Austen-Liegh writes. 'Fashionable as the school has become in one sense it is decidedly democratic, and boys of plebeian origin were to be found, especially among those who sought the benefits of the foundation.' Thus we find parents belonging to the following trades and professions sending their boys to Eton: baker, bookseller, brickmaster, grocer, innkeeper, mercer, upholsterer etc.

Between 1536 and 1540 the monasteries

St George's Chapel has an unbroken history stretching back to its mediaeval foundation. Its beautiful architecture is enhanced by the music of the liturgy, which accompanies the many state occasions connected with the monarchy, and performed by a choir of men and boys established by statute in 1352. The original song-school – the earliest school founded in Windsor – had six chorister boys who were given instruction by one of the vicars. The boys were drawn from local families in the cloisters or the town. The school now has 315 pupils, and accepts both boys and girls. There are 20 choristers who continue the tradition of singing regularly in St George's Chapel both for Sunday services and the regal ceremonies.

were dissolved by order of Henry VIII and where these had schools they were also destroyed. There is no tangible evidence of schools in the town of Windsor but a few snippets of information are available. In 1571, Roger Ascham, a resident of Windsor, was commissioned by Sir Richard Sackville to write a book on the teaching of children to read, write and speak. Books were not readily available and only the Bible or the New Testament could be found in the more wealthy homes. Some historians suggest that there was a higher level of literacy among women of the Elizabethan period than at any time until the 19th century. The wife of an educated man who had learned to read and write might gather her own and other children into a class in order to pass on her knowledge.

But until the early 18th century the main provision of education in the area was limited. There must have been Dame schools and junior clergy have always been available to supplement their meagre incomes by tutoring individual pupils or small groups of boys. For the Royal Family and nobility there would be tutors and a governess for the girls. From 1606 all schoolmasters were required to be licenced by the Bishop and in 1688 Widow Stileman was ordered to appear before the Arch Deanery Court for running a school in Windsor without a licence. So it seems that the Church firmly controlled what passed for education in the 17th century.

There was little enthusiasm for educating the poor. It was generally felt that if the poor were educated, they would come to despise their lot in life and become rebellious. As the area was mostly agricultural there was not the impetus for acquiring literacy, although the route by which a man became a master craftsman, through apprenticeship, was acknowledged.

Basic numeracy and literacy were clearly needed if one was to become a freeman, a trader, and eventually a member of the fraternity.

In the early 18th century, attitudes began to change and the more enlightened felt that children should be taught to read in order that they could read their Bibles. At the end of the previous century, in 1698, came the Society for the Promotion of Christian Knowledge, the aim of which was to spread the Christian message throughout the population. Schools started by this organisation were usually linked to the parish church which sustained them by church collections. The establishment of the 'charity schools' was the bedrock on which the future of universal education would grow and flourish. By 1700 the charity schools were so numerous that an inspector of charity schools was appointed.

Some benefactors left land and money for founding and maintaining such a school. In 1701 John Porter left money in his will to a school which was in Priest Street (St Albans Street).

This was followed in 1704 by the will of Mary Barker who left £360 for the purchase of lands the rents of which would provide the wages of a schoolmaster or school-

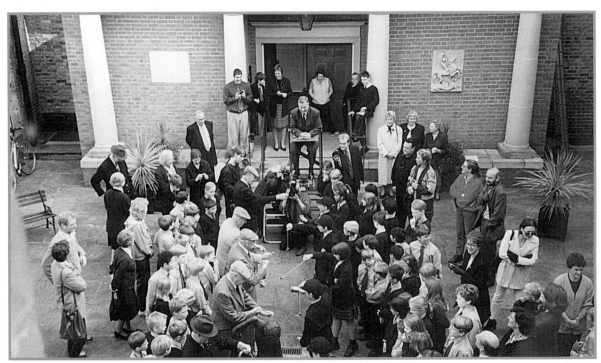

A conker match between the pupils of St George's School and the military knights in 1999.

King Henry VI, whose statue can be seen in the Eton School yard, founded Britain's most famous school in 1441. The building of Eton College commenced with the chapel – a beautiful building which was intended by its royal founder to be even larger and grander than the present one with its dimensions more resembling a cathedral than a school chapel. The foundation was to combine a college for secular priests, a charity school for boys and an almshouse. From the beginning a number of 'poor scholars' were to be boarded, fed and clothed as well as educated. This number of 25 was increased to 70.

One of the more important provisions of the statutes was the granting of free instruction in grammar to an indefinite number of boys from any part of the world. Twenty of these commoners were specially privileged as being members of the nobility and gentry and were allowed to live in college; humbler boys were allowed to dine in hall and hence the name Commensals was applied to all commoners.

The Wars of the Roses were a perilous time for the college. In 1471, King Henry was murdered in the Tower of London, and every year, to mark the anniversary of the king's death, representatives from Eton and King's College, Cambridge, place white roses and lilies in the cell where he died and on his tomb in St George's Chapel.

One reason for its fame was the number of distinguished men who were educated there. Eton College played its role in national affairs as boys were educated to become statesmen, lawyers, military leaders and country gentlemen.

In 1891 total admission reached 1,000 boys, and the numbers in Eton had become so large and boys packed into the chapel so tightly that some fainted in the crush. Today, Eton College has 1,290 pupils aged 13-18 years who are all boarders.

mistress. Children would be taught to read their Bibles and the Book of Common Prayer. Girls would also be taught to knit and sew, useful skills with which they could support themselves.

The Bishop of Salisbury granted a corner of the churchyard on which was built in 1726 a handsome red-brick building which was 'The Royal Free School'.

The provision of schooling for army children followed from the influence of the Duke of York, who as Commander in Chief of the British Army, was keen to promote literacy amongst the NCOs. In 1803 the

This is from a coloured illustration on the tomb of Sir Henry Savile in Merton College Chapel. Sir Henry Savile was the Provost of Eton and the Warden of Merton College, Oxford.

Duke of York School in Chelsea was founded under his auspices and had 150 boys and 50 girls (by 1811 there were 1,792 boys and girls). Its aim was to educate the children of NCOs and soldiers and by 1811 the Duke of York had persuaded the Government to provide schools in all the regiments. It is clear that by 1826 every regiment in Windsor would have its own school with a schoolmaster sergeant. Soldiers' children were given the opportunity to acquire basic numeracy and literacy, although not all parents took the opportunity to have their children educated probably because even the modest fees of 4d for one child and 6d for two and 8d for three or more children were beyond their means. By 1870 tuition fees for army children had been abolished.

The 19th century saw the proliferation of a bewildering number of schools, some of which lasted only a few years. The expansion of schooling was led by the Nonconformist religions which established Sunday schools in some of the poorest areas of Windsor. They were motivated by the desire to give children a Christian education and raise the moral standards of the poor which had sunk to the the level of the festering slums in which they lived.

Some schools also had to provide food and clothing for the very poor. There was nothing in the least bit egalitarian about the schools, if anything, they reinforced the class differences which already existed in British society and children from different social classes did not mix at school.

The words of the Victorian hymn:

> The rich man in his castle,
> The poor man at his gate,
> God made them high or lowly
> And ordered their estate.

made it all too clear that you belonged in a certain class of society and there you should stay.

The very poor went to the 'ragged schools' and as their name implies the children wore rags. Other schools included the charity schools, the national schools and the church schools. The free places at the charity schools were often awarded to the children of artisans and tradesmen.

By the end of the 19th century there was universal education available for all children. Although there was no grammar school there was a wide range of church and private schools including academies for young gentlemen and seminaries for young ladies.

At the beginning of the 20th century came the passing of the Education Act of 1902. The Windsor Boys' School which although it charged fees did admit boys from the church elementary schools on 'free places' and also 'county scholars' who had been successful in county competitive examinations. Similar education for the girls had to wait until 1920 when Windsor Girls' School was opened.

In the 1970s came the Comprehensive Education Act which changed the provision of education throughout the country. In Windsor the 11-plus ceased to be a compulsory examination for the selection of children for the grammar schools. All the state secondary schools in Windsor became comprehensive schools and offered a non-selective education to all children up to the age of 16.

At the beginning of the 21st century Windsor, unlike neighbouring towns, divided schooling into a three-tiered system which provides 'first schools' for children aged 5-9 years, 'middle schools' for children aged 9-13 years and 'senior schools' for pupils aged 13-16 or 18 years. There were 13 primary schools, four middle schools and two senior schools, one for boys and one for girls which provided state education for 5,252 pupils.

There was also a private sector which included fee-paying schools such as Upton House School which was founded in 1936 and educated boys and girls up to the age of seven and then girls only up to age 11.

The Brigidine School was established in 1948 as the Brigidine Convent by the Congregation of the Sisters of Saint Brigid but teaches children of all denominations. It too takes boys as well as girls up to the age of seven years and then girls are educated up to 18.

A boys preparatory school (St John's Beaumont) is situated on Crimp Hill, Old Windsor, and takes boys from 4-13 as day boys or boarders. It was founded in 1888 by the Society of Jesus.

St George's School, Windsor Castle, is a preparatory school specialising in music and from which the famed St George's Choir draws its choristers.

Three schools that began independently went on to merge into the 'Free schools'. The schools that merged were, the 'Free' or 'Charity schools', the 'Ladies school' and the 'National school'. Their history begins with the bequest of Mary Barker who in 1704 left the sum of £350 in her will to buy lands in trust for the maintenance of a sober, pious and able Protestant to teach poor children to read. The 40 boys and 30 girls were taught reading, writing and arithmetic and the girls were also instructed in sewing and knitting. At first the children were probably taught in the church but in 1725 a fine new brick school was built in the corner of the churchyard.

At the beginning of the 18th century John Porter left money in his will for a school in Priest Street (now St Albans Street) and there was also a school, governed by the deans and canons of St George's Chapel, called Queen Anne's School. The trustees of these schools decided to amalgamate and in 1859 the Windsor Royal Free and Industrial School was established and free education for 35 boys and 35 girls was provided. Other pupils at the school were required to pay school pence.

In 1859 the Royal Free School and the national school amalgamated and moved into this building which was built on Bachelors' Acre and opened in 1862. The old school building near the parish church became the Masonic Hall. The new school was renamed the Royal Free and Industrial School. In the 1980s the younger pupils joined St Edwards' Royal Free Ecumenical Middle School and the older children moved into a new building in Bourne Avenue that was called the Princess Margaret CE Royal Free School. This school closed in 2000, thus ending nearly 300 years of school history.

An old print shows a row of cottages (1815–50) that are on the same site as the present Clewer Green School which was previously known as the Harcourts' Charity. Lady Harcourt left £500 to be invested for the poor of Clewer Parish and a copy of an extract of her will can be seen on the wall of the belltower in St Andrew's Church.

Clewer Green School, Hatch Lane. This photograph that was taken in 2002 shows how the present school has evolved from the original Harcourts' Charity. It is now a Church of England primary school and has places for 180 pupils aged 5-9 years.

Young musicians of St Mark's School in the mid-19th century. The story of St Mark's School begins with the forming of a choir at Holy Trinity Church by Stephen Hawtrey who was a master at Eton College. He was persuaded to open a school where music would play a significant part in the education of its pupils. A cottage was rented and a master, Charles Morgan from St Mark's Training College, was appointed. The boys and their master would meet at the early morning service and then walk back together to the school where they shared breakfast before starting lessons.

The school opened with 19 pupils but such was the demand that extra cottages were added and the number of boys increased to 50. Stephen Hawtrey possessed advanced views on education and wanted his school to serve 'a class of the community which was lower than that which is reached by St Mark's School'. He opened a subscription list for a bigger school which was headed by Queen Victoria. The new school opened in Alma Road on 25 April 1862 with Stephen Hawtrey as the headmaster. Although it began as a day school, a boarding house was added in 1870.

In 1906 St Mark's School amalgamated with the United Service College. This picture shows a guard of honour for the German emperor on 11 November 1907. The college had been founded at Westward Ho! in north Devon where its most famous pupil, Rudyard Kipling, had based his stories of *Stalky & Co.*

The merger of the two schools did not prevent growing financial problems and they approached the Imperial Service College Trust, whose objectives included helping with the education of the sons of officers in the armed forces. The school became the Imperial Service College and in 1920 it bought the estate which included Clewer Manor and there opened the junior school in 1922.

In 1931 a school hall was erected and named after the regiment, King Edward's Horse. Besides the King Edward's Horse Hall, another new building, the Kipling Memorial Building, was erected and occupied on 29 September 1939. But the school did not survive the war years and in 1942 it amalgamated with Haileybury School. The junior school was then renamed Haileybury Junior School. The site of the Haileybury Junior School, which included Clewer Manor, was sold to developers in 1999.

William Riley, who lived in The Hermitage, Clewer, erected a chapel and a small house for a resident priest next to his home in Hermitage Lane. The priest said Mass for Catholic soldiers stationed in Windsor and also ran a small school for their children. In 1898, St Edward's Free Elementary School for Mixed and Infants opened in Dorset Road, Windsor.

Class 4, St Edward's RC School, Dorset Road, Windsor, 1930. In 1828, Father John Wilkinson arrived in the town. He felt that the children of the Catholic poor were being deprived of a spiritual education. Initially, Father Wilkinson organised a small school at his house, for which there was a schoolmaster. A congregation of 200 Catholics, including some 60 soldiers, opened a subscription list for the provision of both the school and a church. Eventually, classes were transferred to the sacristy of the church, under the tutelage of a Miss Hunt.

It was Father Loginotto, an educated and cultured figure (he was chairman of the Windsor Education Committee in 1902) who instigated the building of a new school in Dorset Road. This opened in November 1898 with 59 pupils and 2 schoolmistresses, the Misses Butterly. In April 1965, the infants' school opened in Parsonage Lane and in 1968 all the pupils moved to the new school. In 1986 the St Edward's Royal Free Ecumenical Middle School in Parsonage Lane was opened after the merger of St Edward's RC Middle School and the Royal Free Middle School.

St Stephen's School in the early years of the 20th century. By 1863, on the western edge of the town, a new community had developed in the area around Bexley Street, Clewer Lane and Clewer Fields. It was a poor and overcrowded place with an unsavoury reputation, so the nuns from the Convent of St John the Baptist decided that it needed their missionary work. In less than a decade the nuns had opened five schools in the new parish of St Stephen's.

The first was St Stephen's Mission School which began in a derelict cottage in Clewer Fields. The first pupils were so dirty and ragged that they had to be washed first before lessons could begin; such children were accustomed to sleeping rough and foraging for their food. By 1867, gifts of money had enabled the sisters to buy land on which to build a mission house that housed a chapel on the ground floor and the school on the upper floors. The first school was for the very poorest of children whose parents could not afford the penny or twopence charged per week at the church schools and who were too dirty or unkempt to be welcomed at these schools. The nuns extended their teaching to those whose parents could pay a small amount each week. This was the beginning of the St Stephen's National School for Boys, Girls and Infants. The Clewer Sisters also started St Stephen's Girls' Middle School for the daughters of tradesmen and shopkeepers.

The infant class in 1915 of Holy Trinity School, Clewer (formerly, St Anne's). As there are 60 children squeezed into the classroom it is probably a picture of the whole school. Nearly all the girls are wearing their pinafores. The pupils are holding up specimens of leaves which were probably collected during a nature ramble.

St John's Beaumont at Crimp Hill, Old Windsor, was founded in 1886 by the Society of Jesus, a Catholic religious order primarily concerned with education. It was built for 60 boys but by 2000 it had 360 pupils aged 3-13 years which included full boarders, weekly boarders and day boys.

A section of the school photograph of Windsor Boys' School taken in the 1930s. Raymond South, a master (second from right, second row from bottom) and Maurice Bond, then a boy (second from left, third row) both became distinguished local historians. The school was founded in 1908 near Holy Trinity Church and moved to its present site in Maidenhead Road in 1938.

The name of the Eton Porny School is a corruption of the name Marc Antoine Pyron du Martre, a Frenchman who anglicised his name to Mark Antony Porny after he arrived in England in 1754. He taught French to the boys in Eton College and on his death in 1802 he left his estate for the establishment of a school. There was already a Sunday School in Eton, founded by Provost William Roberts in 1790, and it was to extend the work of this original school that Mark Porny wished his money to be dedicated. His family in France challenged his will and it was not until 1813 that a school was opened for 60 boys and 60 girls who were admitted at seven years and left at 13 for the girls and 14 for the boys.

By 1863 the building was too small as the school had 120 boys, 90 girls and 90 infants and it moved to its present site. In 2001 the school, which is now a CE first school, has 138 pupils aged 5-11 years.

Eton College boys doff their straw boaters on the Thames on 4 June 1999, Founders' Day.

SLUMS AND STEAM TRAINS: THE VICTORIAN RENEWAL OF WINDSOR AND ETON

Never was there such a sink of impurity as my native town…
the Goswells, which in winter were flooded, were in spring
summer and autumn, pestilent with black ditches… In the
Bachelors' Acre the 'little victims' played by the side of a great
open cesspool, kept brimming and overflowing by drains
disgorging from every street.
(Charles Knight, *Passages of a Working Life*)

WHEN Victoria came to the throne in June 1837 after the death of her uncle, William IV, Windsor was still a small but prosperous market town. The expensive reconstruction of the castle, which had begun in the reign of George IV, was completed just before the young Queen ascended the throne. The Victorian period saw the expansion of the British Empire; the largest empire the world has ever known. Queen Victoria made the mediaeval castle her principal royal residence and entertained the many heads of state who came to visit her. The pageantry of the court and the marching of the soldiers brought the tourists to the town. Windsor became not only the focal point of the life of the nation but also the centrepiece of the Empire.

But if we take a look at the town behind the grandeur of the Court a different picture emerges. Described by Jonathan Swift in the 18th century as 'a delightful situation but the town is scoundrel', by the time Victoria came to the throne the dirtiness and overcrowding of the town had grown worse. The area known as Bier Lane – supposedly named thus because of the practice of carrying corpses down to the river for despatch to the burial ground at Clewer – had degenerated to a warren of mean buildings, utterly lacking in any form of sanitation with backyard refuse heaps draining through the houses when the river flooded. The notorious Clewer ditch which was subject to frequent flooding traversed the area.

The general impression which assailed the visitor was one of squalor; it was described in detail in a report by Edward Cresy, Superintendent Inspector of the Board of Health in 1838, who reported on the open cesspools, the garbage heaps, the sewage which stagnated in the ditches and the smells and overcrowding which led inevitably to disease and death. Of every 100 children born, 15 died in their first year, 32 before they were five and 42 before they were 15.

From the local paper, the *Windsor Express*, we catch glimpses of a seedier side of Royal

By the time this portrait was painted, the Queen, who had worn unrelieved black since the death of Albert, the Prince Consort, was wearing a white cap and adding white frills to her dress.

This picture is from the painting in the Windsor Guildhall called *A View of Windsor High Street and Market* by William Westall *c.*1830. It was painted seven years before Victoria became queen and shows the mounted cavalry on its way to the castle.

This scene was photographed by George Henton towards the end of Queen Victoria's reign. He shows the High Street to be even more crowded with street traders selling their wares direct from baskets or makeshift stalls.

Windsor. There are references, for example, to the 'gaming and other disorderly houses' and to a meeting held at the Guildhall for the purpose of taking into consideration the most prompt means of suppressing the practice of gambling, which had reached an unprecedented extent in the town.

In the year immediately before Victoria came to the throne we are told that the streets 'swarmed with prostitutes and beggars'.

Windsor was a garrison town with two barracks housing one infantry and one cavalry regiment. The soldiers and the poor helped to keep over 30 taverns and 20 beer shops in business along with the thriving breweries. It is hardly surprising that intemperance and violence were part of life in the overcrowded and degrading slums. With poverty went prostitution and it was the plight of the destitute 'fallen women' that moved Harriet Monsell to found the House of Mercy and the Convent of St John the Baptist in Clewer.

The situation began to improve with the passing of the Public Health Act in 1848, although a certain apathy pervaded the corporation when the matter of the state of the town drains needed some resolution. Their attitude could be read in their statement 'unnecessarily extravagant and infinitely beyond the means of the inhabitants' which followed any discussion for improvements.

The town council, however, were enthusiastically diligent about their Loyal Addresses to visiting Royalty. Between 1852–74, the mayor and corporation welcomed no less than 11 royal visitors including Napoleon III and Empress Eugénie, the Shah of Persia and the Tsar of all the Russias. Decorative arches for the carriages to pass under were a feature of this period and the corporation encouraged the townsfolk to decorate the houses and streets. Lavish illuminations were all part of the show and gas lighting and oil lamps were lit in abundance and fire precautions seemed not to be a priority.

When the Prince of Wales brought his prospective bride (Princess Alexandra of Denmark) to Windsor in 1863, the rain fell continuously but a great crowd welcomed her. The inevitable triumphal arch was erected in Thames Street and the mayor, already soaked, wisely decided not to read out the Loyal Address and threw it into the carriage thus foregoing his coveted opportunity to speak to a royal princess.

By the middle of the 19th century, Windsor ceased to be a small sleepy country town as the advent of the railways changed it from a rural backwater to a tourist attraction within reach of a now mobile public.

The council having shown very little reforming zeal in its apathetic efforts to clean up the town was galvanised into action on the matter of the railway and the opposition to it by both Eton College and the Crown. Dr Edward Craven Hawtrey, the headmaster of Eton College, supported by the teaching staff foresaw the disciplinary difficulties with their pupils. The Crown, which owned most of the land needed for the railway, was unhappy about the effect of the smoke on its newly furbished walls and the intrusion of its privacy. The conflict between the Crown and college on one hand and the railway companies on the other was one between conservatism and progress. The townsfolk and tradesmen wanted the railway. They could see how a town prospered with advent of the railway age but they all had to live through the endless debates and arguments.

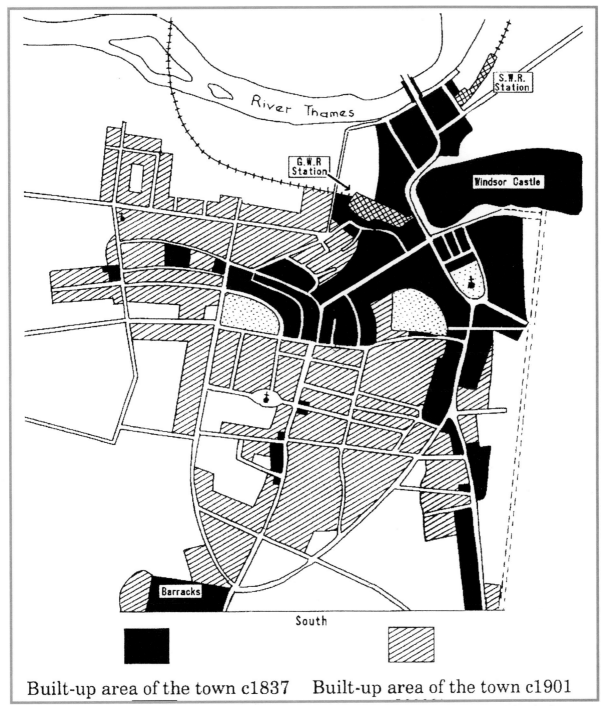

Built-up area of the town c1837   Built-up area of the town c1901

The diagram shows the huge growth of the town from the beginning of the reign of Queen Victoria until her death in 1901. (Judith Hunter)

But by the end of 1849 Windsor had obtained two branch lines and two railway stations, one on Riverside and one under the walls of the castle, the outcome of one of the bitterest conflicts in railway history; a story of rivalry, antagonism, prejudice and vested interests.

The money which the rival railway companies were prepared to invest resulted in the clearances of some of the terrible slums, particularly those which clustered beneath the walls of the castle. Trade, particularly the transport of goods by rail instead of the river, enriched the tradesmen. With rising prosperity went the building of new homes such as those in the districts of Gloucester Place for the middle classes and Bexley Street for the respectable labouring class. However, the housing for the poor was still unsatisfactory, with the exception of the Prince Consort Cottages which were intended as a model of responsible home building. The new housing and roads gave Windsor its present Victorian look and with the arrival of the railway, with its fast access to London, Windsor became a suburban town.

The Victorian era was a religious, churchgoing period and the town reflected this as two new parishes were created along with eight other places of worship. These joined the parish church of St John, the Congregational Chapel in William Street and the Wesleyan Chapel in Peascod Street. At Holy Trinity, known as the garrison church, soldiers marched to church parade every Sunday. The Catholics built St Edward's for the increasing Catholic population and the many RC soldiers, to replace the small chapel at the Hermitage in Hermitage Lane.

Population had grown. The 1851 census shows that the population of Windsor was calculated as 11,217 including 988 military. Following the 1867 Reform Act, Clewer and parts of Eton were included and population stood at 17,281. In 1901 the whole population of Windsor, was 20,301.

Services such as gas and water were still in the hands of private enterprise but at the first quarter of the century the *Windsor Express* comments: 'As respects the improvement of the town generally the introduction of gas is decidedly the greatest which has been known for centuries'. The quality of drinking water available to the people was of a questionable standard. The waterworks were situated in Eton and medical men urged the corporation to effect some improvement in the standard of the town's water supply but it was not until 1888 that the waterworks were acquired by the corporation. But this was too late to prevent outbreaks of waterborne diseases such as cholera and typhoid in 19th-century Windsor, the most famous casualty being the Prince Consort himself.

There was no organised police force at the beginning of Victoria's reign. There was a night constable and six watchmen who had power to arrest vagrants and disorderly persons but this was inadequate protection for an increasing population. With the passing of the Municipal Reform Act in 1835 the council became responsible for the raising of a full-time police force. The Charity Commissioners allowed the Old Workhouse in Sheet Street to be sold to the council for use as a Police Station and lock-up.

All was not doom and gloom in Windsor throughout this period. The arts flourished under the patronage of the Royal Family. The Queen was responsible for the foundation of the Royal Albert Institute in memory of the Prince Consort which was founded to promote the study of literature, science and the fine arts. The children of the sovereign, especially Princesses Helena, Louise and Beatrice and Prince Leopold all supported and encouraged interest in music and the arts. The century saw the foundation of many such societies and the growing interest in sports also led to several sports clubs being founded.

The greatest gift Queen Victoria gave to

people of Windsor was her encouragement of her husband's interest in the welfare of the town. Albert was appointed high steward of the town and took his responsibilities seriously especially in his role as president of the Royal Society for Improving the Condition of the Poor. If Albert had lived longer his legacy would doubtless have been greater and it is a sad irony that it was probably a strain of the lethal bacteria which was endemic in the town that caused his death, a town which he tried so hard to help.

Across the river the townsfolk of Eton would have welcomed a railway but their opinions went unheard. The college was the biggest employer and the poor were dependent on its charitable donations. The coming of the railways was dominated by the objections put forward by the headmaster of the college and as most of the land required for the railway belonged either to the Crown Estates or Eton College, the college had huge power to make decisions which would affect the townsfolk. The headmaster, Dr Hawtrey, supported by his staff, took the view that the discipline of their boys was at stake: 'The boys would travel up to London for vice… they would fight with the navigators… they would throw stones at the train and injure the passengers.'

Moreover, in the government, committees which judged the merits of the various railway schemes put before them, many of the adjudicators were Old Etonians and supported the stance of their old school. So the arguments raged on.

When the scheme was at last accepted, the GWR paid £246 as compensation for the extinction of 'lammas' rights on the land taken over by the railway in 1849. This seems a paltry amount compared with the huge

This picture of the Reading-London coach passing Windsor and Eton in the 1820s shows the most comfortable way of travelling before the railway age.

The first Windsor and Eton Central Railway Station opened on 8 October 1849, was a timber structure typical of the work of Isambard Kingdom Brunel, designer and builder of the Great Western Railway. Queen Victoria and her court used the station to travel to Paddington as early as 23 November 1849. The GWR obtained permission in 1897 to build a new station to celebrate the Queen's Diamond Jubilee.

sum of £85,000 which was secured by the Crown Estates from the railway companies. Once the railway was accomplished, a college watchman was required to patrol alongside the railway viaduct where it passed near the college. The railway did not have the dramatic effect in Eton as it did in Windsor where the notorious slums were swept away and new buildings appeared.

The people of Eton were all too conscious of the castle, which loomed over the skyline and their lives. The Queen would regularly sweep through the town on her way from Slough to Windsor. A succession of carriages, accompanied by a mounted escort, passed down the High Street and over the bridge. The people and tradesmen would put out their bunting and the college boys shouted and cheered and ran beside the Queen's carriage all the way to the castle.

The arrival of the railway changed the face of Windsor so that it became cleaner and less disreputable. Fortunately, the disfigurements of the industrial age had been kept out of the town and the now mobile public flocked to the free spectacle of regal pomp and military pageantry. Windsor and Eton had moved into the tourist age.

South Western Railway Terminus at Windsor & Eton Riverside Station. The picture is interesting because it shows the flag man regulating the crossing as a horse and rider wait to cross the lines. On the right-hand side of the picture the disc signal apparatus can be seen. Above the roof of the station is the tower where the look out man would watch for Queen Victoria as she was driven down towards the station from the castle.

This grand entrance to the Great Western Railway was part of the rebuilding plans intended for Queen Victoria's Diamond Jubilee. Station Approach was once the infamous George Street which housed many of the town brothels.

A poster announcing excursions run by the Great Western Railway in 1897 from Windsor to Ascot for the racing. There had been a proposal to build a railway between Windsor and Ascot which had obtained Royal Assent in 1898 and although extra time had been allowed for the completion of a railway by 1912 the GWR had decided to abandon the proposal.

Princess Helena (1846–1923), the fifth
of Queen Victoria's children and the
third daughter. She was only 15 when
her father died and she became an
indispensable secretary to her bereaved
mother. Her father's influence was to
show itself when she spent a great deal
of her adult life caring for the people of
Windsor. In 1866 she married Prince
Christian of Schleswig-Holstein and
they lived for most of their life in
Cumberland Lodge in Windsor Great
Park. Princess Christian, as she was
then known, became concerned with
the welfare of poor children and helped
to establish a nursery. However, her
greatest work was in the field of
nursing where she founded the nurses
training school at 1 and 2 Clarence
Villas. After the death of her eldest son,
Prince Christian Victor, in the Boer
War, the princess bought 3 and 4
Clarence Villas which became a nursing
home in his memory.

This photograph shows the statue of Prince Christian Victor (1867–1900) which commemorates his death in the Boer War and was erected in Thames Street. Prince Christian Victor was the eldest son of Prince and Princess Christian. He died in South Africa in October 1900 just before he was due to return home. This statue of the prince was unveiled at Windsor in November 1903.

Mariquita Tennant, a widow living at The Limes (pictured below) near Clewer Church, took in a destitute young woman, one of many such girls who needed shelter from the appalling conditions which existed in the town. Thus began the work of the Clewer House of Mercy. The women rescued by Mrs Tennant were often victims of the squalid conditions endemic in Windsor at this time. The coming of the railways did nothing to improve the moral climate of the town, as the squalid overcrowded housing, washed through with filth, had to accommodate the railway 'navvies' as well as the overflow of soldiers' families. The beer shops thrived, adding drunkenness and violence to illness and disease.

This portrait is of Harriet Monsell as a young woman. She was installed as the first Superior of the Community of St John the Baptist, Clewer, formed to supervise the work of the House of Mercy.

St Andrew's Hospital was part of the work of the Community of St John the Baptist at Clewer. This photograph shows the sisters by the dovecote in the hospital gardens.

The Clewer House of Mercy was one of the first convents in the Church of England to take up the work of caring for women.

Schools, homes and hospitals founded by the Clewer Sisters		
House of Mercy	1852	the convent and penitentiary for fallen women
St John's Home	1855	orphanage and industrial school for girls
St Andrew's Cottage	1861	a cottage hospital
St Andrew's Hospital	1866	for invalids of both sexes
	1875	children's ward opened
St Andrew's Cottages	1868	almshouses for 12 poor women
St Augustine's Home	1858	a boys home
St Stephen's Mission School	1863	a ragged school
St Stephen's National Schools	c1863	elementary schools for boys, girls and infants
Stephen Middle School	c1863	advanced school for girls
St Stephen's College	1871	Secondary school for daughters of poor clergy and gentry

The quadrangle at St Stephen's High School, Clewer.

Sir Francis Tress Barry (1825–1907) was a wealthy industrialist who had made his fortune in Portuguese copper mining. Like many industrialists of that period he was looking for a country estate preferably with an existing house and surrounded with parkland. St Leonard's Hill had one of the best landscapes money could buy, having a peerless view of Windsor Castle.

In 1876 Barry was created a baron by the King of Portugal and he styled himself Baron Barry of Portugal but he dropped this title in 1889 when Queen Victoria created him a baronet for his services to Windsor. A generous benefactor to many good causes, particularly the infirmary, Sir Francis also served as MP for Windsor between 1890 and 1907.

St Leonard's Hill, Windsor, 1891. By the time this photograph was taken Tress Barry had converted what was a charming Georgian mansion to his idea of a French chateau. This was the nouveau riche style of house building. France was considered to be the centre of fashionable elegance so the architect, Charles Howell, with cheerful ebullience, combined steep and ornate French mansard roofs with an Italianate tower.

Upon entering Sir Francis Tress Barry's mansion the visitor would have been suitably impressed by the grandeur of the magnificent octagonal central hall which was lit by a circular glazed dome. From the hallway a double staircase ascended in three short flights and a fourth flight led into the gallery. Large slabs of Mexican onyx had been imported to line the walls of this gallery and above them hand painted frescoes depicted scenes from Roman and Greek mythology.

The ruins of St Leonard's Hill. Barry's fine mansion did not survive long after World War One. In 1917 Lady Tress Barry died and her son Edward tried to sell the estate but after the war there was no demand for great country houses which required large domestic staffs. Some became schools or nursing homes and it was considered that St Leonard's Hill could convert into a hospital but, as it was without mains water and its sewage drained into cesspits, such a use was not practical.

Only one generation had enjoyed the opulence of this Victorian stylish mansion. Built for an earlier period when there was plentiful labour to service it, the house was essentially doomed when domestic labour became hard to find and it was too grand and too demanding to be adapted to suit a simpler household.

The River Thames froze over in the Great Freeze of 1894.

Windsor and Eton have been regularly flooded by the Thames which resulted in the many insanitary slums of the area. A report to the General Board of Health by Edward Cresy in 1838 called Windsor the most insanitary town in the country. During the 19th century floods were recorded in 1849, 1852, 1873, 1875 and 1894. In 1894 the river rose 9ft and two months later it froze in the Great Freeze.

In 1875, an artist for *The Illustrated London News* sketched these pictures of how the Windsor residents coped with the frequent floods. Punts were used as public transport and where possible temporary bridges were erected. Great ingenuity was used to make sure that deliveries of coal and the post continued with as little delay as possible.

Eton Wick boys gathering wild flowers. It has been suggested that the boys gathered the flowers to sell to the day trippers on the passing river steamers.

The Royal Windsor Tapestry Manufactory was opened in 1876 and closed in 1890. Weavers came from Aubusson in France and wove high-quality tapestries from designs by notable artists of the day. The Tapestry Hall was built in 1882 to house the expanding business which enjoyed the encouragement from the Royal Family. Prince Leopold was the patron but at the time of his sudden death in 1884 the business had begun to suffer acute financial problems due to declining orders. It closed its doors on Christmas Eve 1890. Until 1962 the central hall of the building which once housed the looms was used as a village hall but now the whole building has been converted into self-contained flats.

This picture by George Henton, dated 1895, shows Lizzie Halley feeding her fowls in Eton Court which was built about 1840 and demolished in 1911. It housed about 56 people, several of whom were laundresses. This is now the entrance to Eton car park.

One of the tapestries produced by the Royal Windsor Tapestry Manufactory to a design by Richard Beavis (1824–96) is owned by the Corporation of London. It is 9ft 6ins by 5ft 6ins and cost £200 in 1887. The subject commemorates the opening of the Royal Exchange by Queen Elizabeth and shows her being received by Sir Thomas Gresham, citizen and mercer at the Royal Exchange on 23 January 1571.

APPOINTMENT

Eton floods, 1894.
Eton was at the mercy
of the Thames and
subjected to as much
flooding as Windsor.

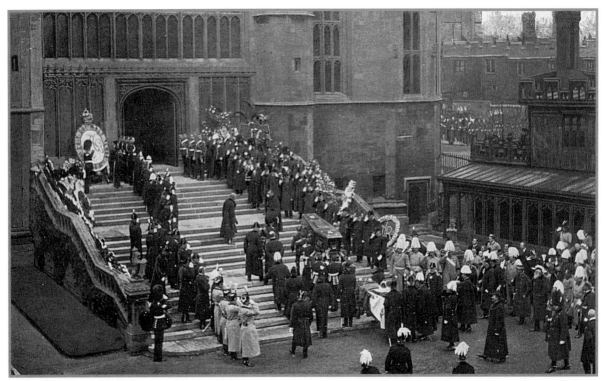

Queen Victoria died at Osborne on the Isle of Wight on 22 January 1901. Her coffin was brought by train to arrive at Windsor's Great Western Station on 2 February. There the funeral cortège passed through Windsor until it finally arrived at St George's Chapel where a service was held. After the service the coffin was taken to the Albert Memorial Chapel where it rested until Queen Victoria was laid beside her beloved Albert in the beautiful Royal Mausoleum.

The maid and children watching the Coldstream Guards marching down Sheet Street are part of the daily spectacle in Windsor in the 1870s. Even quite humble households had a maid and domestic service was the largest employer of female labour in the country.

THE CHANGING FACE: 1901–1939

QUEEN Victoria died in 1901 and having spent a great deal of her widowhood in the town, she was referred to as 'the Widow of Windsor'. Depressingly, the Boer War continued into the new century and its casualties mounted steadily, including one of the Royal Family, Prince Christian Victor, the son of Prince and Princess Christian. However, it was hoped that the new monarch, with his well-known geniality, would lift the spirits of the people and take their minds off the troubles in South Africa. King Edward VII did indeed bring a new spirit of enjoyment to his reign and, although he preferred the lights of London, Windsor was the base for royal shooting parties and the racing at Ascot. Between 1901 and 1909 there were six state visits which took place in Windsor adding entertainment and spectacle to the lives of the townspeople.

Windsor and Eton managed to avoid the industrial strife that occurred in the rest of the country during the Edwardian period. There was little local industry, apart from the breweries, but there was always need for domestic staff at Eton College. After World War One ended in 1918, the development of Slough Trading Estates meant that increasingly, employment became available just a short distance away. The disposal of surplus Army vehicles from the Slough Depot led to the rise of such companies as Windsorian Coaches which were to cater for the emerging leisure travel industry.

Although wages remained low the currency was stable. Differences in the apparel of rich and poor people became less obvious. This was mainly due to the availability of ready-made clothing which was cheaper than bespoke garments. Multiple retailers such as Montague Burton sold good mens' suits at affordable prices and drapers such as Caley's and Daniel's sold women's garments which rivalled the costs of the private dressmakers.

The 1902 Education Act made county councils and boroughs responsible for secondary and technical education and meant that public money was now available for properly paid teachers and a standardised level of education. Windsor Boys' School was founded in 1908 and the Girls' School in 1920. One result of the rising level of education was that the number of books published steadily increased and there was a growing need for a public library which was finally opened in 1933. Moreover, grants became available to send children to the new county schools on a scholarship thus encouraging gifted children to enter the universities. It was as early as 1912 that a university scholarship was awarded to F. Portas, a pupil of Windsor Boys' School.

Windsor is a town bounded by the River Thames to the north and Crown land to the south and east with development available only to the west. At the turn of the century slums still existed and 100 houses in the Goswells were considered unfit for habitation. They were purchased by the National Trust in order to prevent unsuitable development from spoiling the view of the castle. To replace this lost housing stock the council built houses at Clewer Avenue and later at Dedworth. The

River Street slums (formerly Bier Lane) were replaced in 1926 by a car park and public lavatories and more council houses were built in Dedworth, replacing the demolished slums. Private developers built houses in the west of the town but not on the scale which was to accelerate after World War Two. In effect the villages of Dedworth and Clewer became suburbs of the Borough of New Windsor and eventually the boundaries between them became invisible.

There were, however, many visible changes along the river. Alexandra Gardens were opened in 1905, with a bandstand, flower beds, tennis courts and lawns, for families to enjoy themselves. Queen Victoria had already given that part of Home Park between Datchet Road and the river as a place of recreation and it was handed over to the council in 1938. Now it was possible to watch football, rugby, hockey and cricket there and attend the Royal Windsor Horse Show and Dog Show against a backdrop of the castle.

The new popular entertainment of attending the cinema began to take over from other leisure pursuits in the pre-war period. There was a choice of no less that four cinemas one of which eventually reverted to a theatre.

There were few cars on the road in Edwardian days, those that were being owned by the rich. It was quickly proved necessary to tar the roads to eliminate the clouds of dust thrown up by motor traffic and, indeed, the first traffic jam in Windsor

In the background of this picture is Eton College. King Edward VII is boarding his state barge ready to take part in the parade of boats, part of the Eton College celebrations on Founder's Day.

was recorded in 1905 when the king held a garden party at the castle.

Local government at this time was not on the scale it is today. The Guildhall was used mainly for meetings and whichever local solicitor held the position of town clerk had to provide his own office facilities. The foundation stone for a new Municipal Building was laid in 1905 and the completed building, which was finished in 1907, included the fire station, police station and magistrates court.

One of the most important buildings of this period was the new hospital. The old infirmary could no longer cope with rising numbers of patients and there was no room for expansion on the site. Crown land was acquired opposite the Combermere Barracks thanks to the efforts of Prince Christian and the raising of funds from public subscriptions.

Wealthy local business men such as Sir Francis Tress Barry contributed generously to the new hospital named after King Edward VII, which opened in 1909. The increasing population and the pressures of war necessitated the increase in facilities and, eventually, a new nurses' home was built releasing an entire wing to be used for patients. Moreover, assistance with the running costs was provided by a contributory scheme in 1920 of one penny a week for men, a halfpenny from women and young workers. From 1927 a sum of twopence a week would entitle a contributor or his dependents free in-patient or out-patient treatment. This was in fact a voluntary forerunner of the National Health Service founded in 1948.

In the period between the death of Queen Victoria and the beginning of World War Two Windsor had changed its face by demolishing the remaining Victorian slums and replacing them with council housing and private buildings. Education was made available to all its children and the facilities for leisure were vastly improved. Windsor was no longer the fetid slum of the Victorian era but a pretty and prosperous destination for the increasing number of tourists who came by train or in their charabancs for a pleasant day out.

The celebrations on Eton College Founder's Day.

King Edward VII held a garden party at Windsor Castle in 1905 that resulted in Windsor's first traffic jam.

On Sundays, when the weather was fine, the Long Walk was thronged with pedestrians. Women and children were dressed in their best clothes and promenaded up and down the Walk, meeting their friends, seeing and being seen, and generally enjoying the fresh air and sunshine. Before the advent of the car, walking in one of the many open spaces of Windsor, was the main leisure activity for people from all walks of life.

King Edward VII died in 1910. Windsor was the setting for his huge funeral procession.

Interested spectators, many of whom had never seen an aeroplane before, are gathered round E.F. Driver's Farman biplane as it arrived on Monday 11 September 1911 at Windsor. The delivery of the first aerial post commemorated the Coronation of George V. Two days before, on 9 September 1911, the young pilot of the first flight, Gustav Hamel, left Hendon for Windsor in a Bleriot XI racing monoplane in a raging gale. The flight took only 13 minutes for the 19 miles at an average speed of 105mph. Unfortunately, Hamel landed at the wrong place – at Shaw Farm Meadow instead of East Farm, Windsor Castle. Between 9-26 September 1911 over 100,000 envelopes and postcards were flown between Hendon and Windsor marking the beginning of the period when the post took to the skies.

Alexandra Gardens, a favourite place to be on a sunny Sunday afternoon.

A riverside view of the gardens which were named after Queen Alexandra, consort to King Edward VII.

The area of River Street has been cleared of buildings ready to allow space for the town's first car park in 1927.

A group of men gather in Peascod Street in the 1930s. A small group seems to be waiting outside the public house for it to open. The licensing laws at that period meant that premises which sold beer, wine and spirits were much more restricted in their opening hours than in the present day. Another group is studying a newspaper. Are they reading the racing results or the job vacancies? Some men found employment building Imperial Road and others were able to buy postcards from a shop nearby and resell them in Thames Street. The bicycle was the best and cheapest form of transport before the age of the motor car.

Funeral parade for George V.

Many thousands of people visited Windsor Castle on the second day of public view of the royal wreaths and floral tributes to the late King George V. Crowds moved slowly round the mass of flowers which were displayed outside St George's Chapel in January 1936.

One of the first outings that was organised by Reg Try was to take this group of Windsor parish church bellringers on their annual excursion in 1921. After World War One, Reg used his demob money to buy a surplus army vehicle from the Slough depot and fit it out as a bus. Reg and his brother Archie added a roof and a canopy to the former ambulance and started their coach company taking passengers from Windsor to the Ascot races.

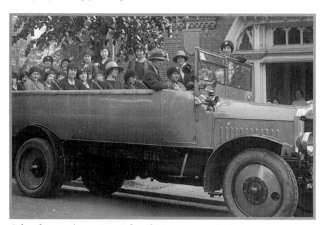

School party in an open charabanc.

Day outings have been popular for all groups from the Victorian period until the present day. The word 'charabanc' entered the language from the French *char-a-banc* and meant 'carriage with benches' and referred to a long, light vehicle with transverse seats looking forward. The French word was used within living memory for motor coaches which took passengers to all manner of places of interest. Reg Try, the owner of Windsorian Coaches, had a thriving business providing coaches for trips to the seaside. Church groups, womens' institutes and schools were amongst his most frequent customers.

WARTIME WINDSOR AND ETON: HOME FRONT AND SANCTUARY FOR LONDONERS

THE drift to war can be traced in the early editions of the *Windsor, Slough and Eton Express* for the year of 1939. By the first week of September of that year it is obvious that there had been plans made months in advance, particularly for the reception of up to 10,000 evacuees from the most exposed parts of London.

Government circles considered that civilian morale would crack almost instantly under air bombardment and that panic-stricken hordes of Londoners would pour out of the shattered capital and into the countryside, where the government had laid contingency plans to turn them back. Plans for the controlled evacuation of four million people from the danger areas before panic set in were already in hand before the declaration of war. It was a planned migration of stupendous magnitude.

On Sunday 3 September at 11.15am, the Prime Minister, Neville Chamberlain announced to the nation 'this country is now at war with Germany'.

The people of Windsor, a quiet suburban town with a grand castle, behaved like the rest of the country. The decision of Parliament and government had been accepted without complaint, all argument was stilled once the war had started. Although many people were expecting an immediate knock out blow what followed was the so called 'phoney war'.

Precautions against air attacks began to take shape. Gas masks were issued to all civilians and were duly carried in their cardboard cases for many months. Street lighting was extinguished on 1 September and the blackout began. Motor cars were forbidden to use their headlights without hoods with the result that deaths on the roads increased alarmingly until the council workers had painted white bands round all the posts and the kerbs. However, many areas of everyday life, such as the cinema – where in Windsor, Shirley Temple was starring in *The Little Princess* – continued largely as normal.

Evacuation was the biggest wartime event to hit Windsor and many people wondered why Windsor had been chosen as a destination for so many evacuees. It was only 20 miles from London and next door to Slough which was an industrial centre with much essential war work. As the evacuation plans got under away the newspapers were full of heart-rending pictures of tearful children, with labels round their necks and their gas mask holders strung from their shoulders, some clutching their teddy bears. In contrast the newsreels tended to show carefree children waving happily goodbye to their parents. It is very difficult to assess the effect of the evacuation on the thousands of children. Newspapers were not allowed to present the true facts if they were likely to damage the morale of the civilian population or affect the fighting forces. The truth was that evacuation caused enormous heartbreak to many families and painful disruption to some host families.

Between 8,000 and 9,000 women and children had arrived from London at the terminus of the Southern Railway. This was considerably less than the number expected because many, at the last moment, refused to leave their homes in the capital. On their arrival the children with their teachers and mothers were given a ration of food consisting biscuits, corned beef, tinned milk and chocolate. A large group of tired and apprehensive evacuees marched to Bachelors' Acre but the others were taken by bus to a central area and then by their billeting officer to their final destinations. By 8.30 in the evening everyone had been found somewhere to sleep. Much has been written of the huge task of evacuating thousands of people from danger zones, but this was hardly as arduous as the problem of finding homes for them in the safe areas.

Children travelled in school groups supervised by their teachers. Many were from Stepney and Poplar and others came from the Clapham area. There was a high proportion of Jewish children, including some Jewish refugees from Europe. Most of the evacuees were placed in pre-arranged homes in Windsor, but some experienced the humiliation of being paraded and then 'selected' by a host family. Although many children were distressed by this, that there were many happy experiences, which survived the trauma, is a tribute to the resilience of the children and the forbearance of their foster parents.

In the days that followed, the new arrivals settled down to a school timetable in which local children attended school in the morning from 9-12.30pm, and the London children, taught by their own teachers, attended the school from 1pm-4.30pm. This did not mean that children were free the rest of the time as outdoor activities were arranged for them, but there were difficulties in finding occupation for them on the dark and wet nights.

The host families were responsible for only food and board of the children and for this they were paid a pittance of 10s a week for one child and 8s 6d each for two. The discipline of the children was not supposed to be their responsibility, though whose it was is not clear. There was an 8pm curfew on the evacuees and presumably the accompanying teachers were to oversee the behaviour of the children. A laundry allowance of 3s 6d a week was added to the billeting grant to cope with the amount of bedwetting amongst the evacuees. It will come as no surprise to most parents that children who are under stress will show it in this manner. Although the local council had imported 1,000 extra beds from Leeds to cope with increase in the child population there were demands from the host families for replacement bedding after their own mattresses had been damaged by evacuee children.

By the beginning of 1940, three out of four evacuees had returned home. There had been no bombing, but there was a great deal of homesickness and, when the government demanded a parental contribution towards the upkeep of the children, the resentful parents took their children home. A new evacuation scheme was launched in February 1940 but it was a complete failure because only one householder in 50 was willing to offer a billet. Soon compulsory powers were required to compel

SATURDAY, JUNE 22, 1940

'BROOMSTICK ARMY' STARTS
TRAINING—AND PARASHOTS
PARADE IN NEW UNIFORMS

Local Defence Volunteers march smartly
from their parade ground in their new
uniforms and full equipment. They are
being trained

Local Defence Volunteers march smartly from their parade ground at the Imperial Service College in Alma Road, wearing their new uniforms and armbands. These men were more fortunate than other units in that they had real rifles to drill with. Other units around the country used broomsticks until proper firearms could be issued. The rifles belong to the Imperial Service College and are used by their cadet corps, so they do not have rifle pins. Frank Radnor, who was a 17-year-old pupil at Windsor Boys' School, was part of the unit which is pictured. They had been formed for six weeks and were mostly ex-servicemen who had fought in World War One. Later the name was changed to the Home Guard.

householders to take evacuees. Many countered this by producing medical certificates to show that the strain of caring for evacuees was too much for their health. Much of the adverse news concerning evacuation was kept out of the newspapers but this did not stop the published account of four homesick children who had attempted to tramp to London, the eldest boy having carried the youngest child all the way to Egham.

The local newspaper was full of upbeat advice under such headlines as 'Business as Usual' and 'Your Emergency Larder'. In the latter the housewife is advised to store certain foods to 'do her bit' to strengthen the nation and show that she will not panic at the last moment.

Business did carry on as usual with the addition of blackout preparations and all the windows being fitted with black curtains or black paper. Sandbags appeared in the High Street, so did many more soldiers. At the castle, the red uniformed guards had donned fighting kit and steel helmets.

In the summer of 1940 civilian soldiers were preparing for an invasion by the German army. Churchill's new Secretary of State for War, Anthony Eden, spoke on the radio about the threat of German parachutists. He then made this appeal:

Since the war began the Government has received countless enquiries from all over the kingdom from men of all ages who are, for one reason or another, not at present engaged in military service, and who wish to do something for the defence of their country. Well, now is your opportunity. We want large numbers of such men in Great Britain, who are British subjects, between the ages of 17 and 65... to come forward now and offer their services... The name of the new Force which is now to be raised will be the Local Defence Volunteers... This name describes its duties in three words... This is a part-time job, so that there is no need for any volunteer to abandon his present occupation... When on duty you will form part of the armed forces... You will not be paid but you will receive a uniform and will be armed...

Before Eden had finished his broadcast, the first volunteers were arriving at the local police stations. In Windsor, men arrived at the police station and signed on for duty. By the following Wednesday 200 had enrolled and applications were still being received. In a broadcast in July 1940, Churchill first referred to the new citizen army as the Home Guard and the name stuck. Many of the first recruits were veterans of World War One. In the period of the nation's greatest peril, the Home Guard was an invaluable asset, releasing thousands of regular troops for other duties, and guarding many of the country's essential services such as the railways. From 1942 they also trained 16 and 17-year-olds who entered its ranks before their call-up. The Home Guard also served as a back up for the Civil Defence services and the anti-aircraft arm many of them serving on AA batteries. And although the invasion never came, the Home Guard went from strength to strength.

The conscription of women was introduced in December 1941, an unprecedented measure which went beyond anything contemplated by Hitler or Stalin. The National Service Act conscripted unmarried women into war work and they had the choice of the uniformed services,

Sergeant Harding with Private Lipscombe, Corporal Blake, Private Cox and Lance-corporal Clark on the parade ground at Dedworth.

such as the WRNS (Women's Royal Naval Service), the ATS (Auxiliary Territorial Service) or the WAAF (Women's Auxiliary Air Force).

They could also work in Civil Defence or make war weapons or work on the land. Married women were wholly exempt as were all women with children under the age of 14. Whatever work women did do it was always paid less than the men in the same occupation. Even when a woman was injured when doing war work, her compensation would be less than that paid to a man.

Windsor and Eton suffered, along with the rest of the country, the hardships of World War Two. There was rationing and restrictions and, for some families, the heartbreak of the loss of their loved ones in the fighting overseas. But perhaps the greatest contribution was the refuge provided by the towns to the many evacuees escaping the London Blitz.

Both Windsor and Eton endured between them 40 air-raids, where 2,000 incendiary bombs and 171 high explosives were dropped. There were nine fatalities and 111 injured in the raids and over a thousand homes were damaged. The first bomb fell on 24 August 1940 and the last bomb on 7 July 1944.

Men of the Dedworth Home Guard are briefed before a night exercise.

Following the broadcast by Anthony Eden in May 1940 in which he called upon men aged between 17 and 65 who were not in military service nor in a reserved occupation, to join their Local Defence Volunteer Force, there was such an immediate and enthusiastic response that the recruiting centres were overwhelmed. Nationwide 1,300,000 men had enrolled. In Windsor the first volunteers arrived at the police station before Anthony Eden had finished his speech, however, in July 1940 the mayor of Windsor was asking for more volunteers as the local force was not up to strength. They were needed for patrol work and for guarding vital positions in the towns in the event of enemy parachutists landing.

This inspection of the Home Guard took place on 25 May 1943 by the Director General. The inspection followed the parade of wartime voluntary units for the 'Wings for Victory' week. The aim of these wartime parades was to raise money for armaments by encouraging people to save money in National Savings and War Bonds. Over £390,000 was invested during 'Wings for Victory' week which was sufficient to buy 78 fighter planes.

A parade of uniformed personnel march through Windsor on 27 May 1943, part of the 'Wings for Victory' week to raise money to buy aircraft.

The graduating officer cadets are ready for inspection after their passing out parade where the salute was taken by the director of the ATS. In the background is the Kipling Memorial Building.

ATS Commandant with cadets. The chief cadet is in the centre.

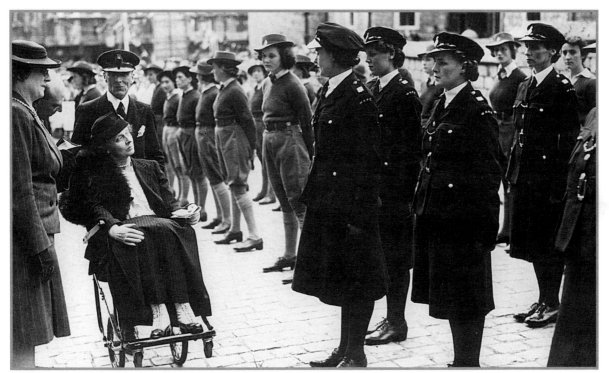

The mayor of Windsor, Mrs Carteret-Carey, is seen here reviewing wartime women's groups in May 1943. In the background is the Women's Land Army. The word 'Army' was a misnomer because although the women were provided with a uniform (green jersey, brown breeches and brown felt hat) they were not subject to army discipline. However, they worked very hard and had very little holiday and none of the privileges of other wartime groups. In the foreground is a group from the Women's Auxiliary Police Corps.

The photograph is of the Windsor Civil Defence Wardens and administrative staff outside their HQ at Trinity Place. In the picture are Joan Epps, secretary to the local controller of Civil Defence; W. Grubb, the chief warden; Marie McKee, accounts clerk; ARP wardens Valentine; Collenette and Cox.

Old Mother Red Riding Boots

CHARACTERS

Lady Christina Sherwood	PRINCESS ELIZABETH
The Honourable Lucinda Fairfax	PRINCESS MARGARET
Mother Hubbard	CYRIL WOODS
Sammy Suction	HUBERT TANNAR
Broker's Man	FREDERICK SMITH
Sir Marmaduke Montmorency	ANNE CRICHTON
Dona Salamanca del Castellianos	MARY MORSHEAD
Fairy	DORIS MARSHALL
Betty Blossom	VIOLET HELPS
Fairflint (the Horse)	DAVID PRESCOTT
	CYRIL STURGES

CHORUS

BETTY ASHTON, EILEEN BUCKLAND, SHEILA COLLINGS, VIOLET HELPS, DORIS MARSHALL, ROSE PEARCE, PHYLLIS PRATLEY, SYLVIA PULLIN, SYBIL STURGES
RONALD ALDRIDGE, JACK ELLIOTT, JUNIOR FINLAYSON, LEONARD HELPS, DENNIS NUTLEY, ERNEST PEARCE, DENNIS QUADLING, KENNETH RICHARDSON, DONALD SIDDLE

BALLET

PRINCESS ELIZABETH, PRINCESS MARGARET, LOUISE COCKCRAFT, ANNE CRICHTON, MARY MORSHEAD, PHOEBE MORSHEAD, JOAN PARKER, DAWN SIMPSON, ANNE VERNEY, CAROLA VERNEY, KARLA WHETHERALL

SCENERY designed and made by
VINCENT KORDA and F. BELLAN
Sound Reproduction by R. H. WOOD of B.B.C.

ACT I
Outside Ye Olde Wishinge Welle Inn

OPENING CHORUS		"Here We Are Again"
CHORUS		
SONG AND DANCE (Lucinda)		"Sing a Song of To-morrow To-day"
DUET AND DANCE		"It's Foolish, but it's Fun"
CHORUS (Christina, Lucinda and Chorus)		"Swinging on a Star"
FINALE, ACT I (Christina, Lucinda and Chorus)		"The Yeomen of England"

INTERLUDE
BALLET

Place : AT THE SEASIDE
Time : THE 1890's
Characters :

THE THREE BELLES	THE NURSE
THE THREE BEAUX	THE SAILOR
THE LITTLE GIRL	THE PHOTOGRAPHER
THE LITTLE BOY	

ACT II
The Glade of the Crystal Stream

SCENA (The Tinies)		"Easter Bunnies"
DUET AND DANCE (Christina and Monty)		"Shepherdess and Beau Brocade"
DUET (Christina and Lucinda)		"Sur le Pont d'Avignon"
FINALE, ACT II		"Sing a Song of To-morrow To-day"

ACT III—Scene 1
On the Road to Ascot

SONG (Sammy)		"My Motter"

ACT III—Scene 2

SONG (Mother Hubbard and Chorus)		"The Quack Quack Song"
TRIO (Christina, Lucinda and Mother Hubbard)		"Get your Guitar"

In December 1944, Joan Epps's uncle, who was the post master at Windsor Castle, obtained two tickets for the Christmas pantomime *Old Mother Red Riding Boots* which was performed in the Waterloo Chamber at Windsor Castle. The performers included the future Queen, then Princess Elizabeth, and Princess Margaret Rose. Princess Elizabeth played the part of Lady Christina Sherwood, one of the leading roles, and Margaret was The Honourable Lucinda Fairfax, the other star part. The King and Queen watched the performance with parental pride, having joined the audience which was made up of Windsor people and service personnel. This is the cast list for the pantomime.

By 1940, the royal family had been evacuated to Windsor Castle and the princesses' governess, Miss Crawford (Crawfie), had been the influence behind the reforming of the 1st Buckingham Palace Girl Guide Company. It would include Princess Elizabeth and Princess Margaret Rose, besides pupils from the Royal School in Windsor Great Park, a few evacuees and children who lived in Windsor Castle. Princess Elizabeth became a Sea Ranger when she was 16 and the picture below shows the future Queen in her uniform as a ranger sitting next to Miss Jeans (a PE instructor) and with Miss Crawford sitting next to Princess Margaret Rose.

Princess Elizabeth is practising her knotting with her fellow Sea Rangers at Frogmore in Windsor Great Park. (Guide Association Archive)

The picture shows the Wisbey family in 1939 when the children Sylvia, Jim and Gerry and their mother Ethel were evacuees in Windsor. They are showing their Aunt Winn (top right) their new school, Braywood, at Oakley Green. At first the family were billeted at a smallholding in Oakley Green. Their father was in the army, and eventually they managed to rent a house in Barry Avenue.

The Wisbey evacuees exploring Windsor have found the ruins of St Leonard's Hill.

At the beginning of World War Two, the St Leonard Estate was purchased by Reg Try of Windsorian Coaches. The lovely mature trees had been compulsory purchased in 1942 and, after their removal, the Ministry of Defence had requisitioned the land as a training ground for the Grenadier Guards. The mansion lost more of its grounds when they were used as part of an assault course. Reg Try managed to keep the soldiers out of his vegetable plot, and the orchard still had a bountiful crop of fruit.

Some Jewish families, fleeing the bombing in London, came to Windsor. Clare Newton and her parents arrived in the town just before the outbreak of war and as the bombing of the East End increased, Clare's grandmother and her great aunts joined them in their house in Barry Avenue. After Clare's father was killed in the fighting in Italy, her mother fell ill and died in hospital in 1945, after which her grandmother, Boba, brought her up. When in 1939 a group of girls from Stepney Green School, East London were evacuated to Windsor, Clare was able to join them for their kosher meals which were served in a wooden building attached to the Thames Hotel. A temporary synagogue was also provided.

Clare Newton's grandmother, Boba, keeping up to date with the news in early post-war Britain.

In 1989 a party of former Windsor evacuees gathered at Eton and Riverside Station for a reunion. This was the station where they had arrived to escape the London Blitz. In the picture they are wearing their labels which identified them to the authorities responsible for their billetting. Pictured above are (front): Anne Thelwell (née Silver), Marion Hellmuth (Complin), and Sylvia Collier (Wisbey). (Back): John Carlton, Vera Levy (Silver), Mary Turner (Barnes), Connie Glanville (Dell), Doreen Crowhurst (Foster) and Gerry Wisbey.

The Willows was the home of Lady Dhunjibhoy Bomanji, the wealthy widow of Sir Dhunjibhoy who was a generous benefactor to Windsor between the wars. The Willows housed evacuated families at the beginning of the war. Lady Dhunjibhoy had gone to live in Harrogate and had donated two of her six Rolls-Royces for the Windsor Air Raid Precautions. There was a desperate shortage of petrol during the war so, as far as she was concerned, the cars would have been redundant for the duration.

Britain had to become self-sufficient and every piece of spare ground was turned over to cultivation. Even the golf courses went under the plough. The slogan 'Dig for Victory' was coined in 1939 and people dug up their beautiful lawns to turn them into vegetable gardens. Even Windsor Great Park had a healthy crop of cabbages. Back gardens came to resemble miniature farms crammed with chicken runs and rabbit hutches.

Good, cheap and plentiful food was supplied by the chain of British Restaurants, run by local authorities and subsidised by central government. By September 1943 there were over 2,000 British Restaurants serving 600,000 meals a day at about 1s (5p) a head.

BOROUGH OF NEW WINDSOR

The Minister of Food desires that every man, woman and child should be in a position to obtain at least one hot nourishing meal daily at a reasonable cost. Accordingly, the Windsor Corporation has pleasure in announcing the opening of its

BRITISH RESTAURANT

AT

127, Peascod Street

WINDSOR, on

MONDAY, 1st SEPTEMBER, 1941

(Hours of Admission : 12 noon to 2 p.m. each weekday)

CHARGES :

MAIN COURSE	8d.
DITTO (Larger Portion)	10d.
DITTO (Children)	4d.
SWEET	2d.
TEA OR SOUP	1d.

J. W. HAMBIDGE, *Town Clerk*

Luff & Sons Ltd., Printers, 47, St. Leonard's Road, Windsor

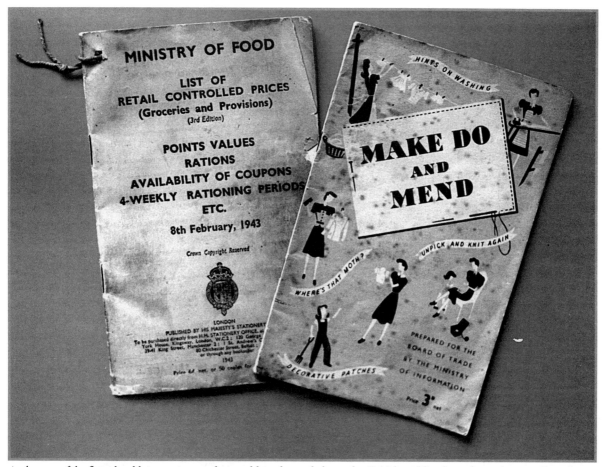

A shower of leaflets, booklets, posters and pamphlets descended on the British public throughout the war. Even home dressmaking which was always a popular hobby became a patriotic duty. The aim of the above booklet was to show readers how to turn their old clothes into bright new garments and to save their clothing coupons. The actual food rations which were allowed during the war years are set out in this page from the Ministry of Food booklet.

BACON — S. R. & O. 1941, Nos. 296, 864 1942, No. 2147

Description or Cut	Maximum Retail Price — Unsmoked per lb. (s. d.)	Smoked per lb. (s. d.)
1. Uncooked and Boneless (in slices or pieces):—		
Middle	2 0	2 1
Back	2 3	2 4
Streak or Belly:—		
Thick	1 8	1 9
Thin	1 4	1 5
Gammon or Ham	2 3	2 3
Prime Collar	1 9	1 9
Fore-end or Shoulder	1 8	1 8
Ulster Roll (including Long Clear):—		
Shoulder-end	1 8	1 8*
Middle Cut	2 0	2 1*
Ayrshire Style Rolled Bacon (Skinless):—		
Middle Cut	2 2	—
Shoulder-end	1 10	—
Gigot	2 5	—
2. Uncooked and Boneless		
Whole Belly	1 4	5.
Uncooked and with Bone:—		
Whole Wiltshire Cut Side	1 7	1 8
Whole Three-quarter Side	1 8	1 9
Whole Spencer	1 7	1 8
Whole Middle	1 8	1 9
Whole Back (cut in the U.K.)	1 11	2 0
Whole Back (cut outside U.K.)	1 10	1 11
Whole Streak	1 3	1 4
Whole Gammon or Ham	1 7	1 8
Whole Fore-end or Square Shoulder without Blade Bone	3.	4
Whole Fore-end or Square Shoulder with Blade Bone	1 3	1 4
Whole Collar without Blade Bone	1 7	1 8
Whole Collar with Blade Bone	1 6	1 7
Picnics	1 2	1 3
Bacon Trimmings (Boneless)	10d. per lb.	

* This is also the price f...

Continued next page.

BACON—...ued

Description or Cut	Maximum Retail Price (s. d.)
5. Cooked, Boneless and with Skin:—	
Streak or Belly in slices or pieces	2 4
Whole	1 11.
6. Cooked, Boneless and Skinless:—	
Gammon or Ham in slices or pieces	3 4
Whole	2 7
7. Cooked, Bone in and Skinless:—	
Gammon and Ham, Whole	2 3
8. Cooked, Boneless in Tins:—	
Gammon or Ham	1 10½ (gross for net)

On a sale of uncooked bacon from which the skin has been removed, the above prices other than those specified for Ayrshire Style Rolled Bacon (Skinless) may be increased by 2d. per lb.

BREAD† S. R. & O. 1943, No. 42:
1. Maximum Retail Price of Bread is 2¼d. per lb. (except under licence).
2. A loaf weighing 1 lb. may be sold at 2½d.
3. The price of Vienna bread, rolls and baps, is not controlled.
4. Speciality bread, rye bread or malt bread may be sold free of price control provided the retailer has available for sale National Bread.
5. Wholemeal Bread, in the production of which no national flour has been used, may be sold under licence by "Health Food Stores" at a price not exceeding 3¼d. per lb.

CAKE (Flour Confectionery, etc.) S. R. & O. 1942, No. 2103
The maximum retail price of any cake is 1s. 6d. per lb., but the price charged if over 1s. per lb. must not exceed 3 times the cost of the ingredients.

No additional charge may be made for wrapper or container.

See page 38 for special price areas

This advertisement is definitely showing its age. Created during a period when the position of women was undergoing profound changes it attempts to solve a dilemma which both men and women were passing through. The advertisement strives to portray a familiar steamed pudding but a tin of the required shape was not available at that time.

PICTURED RIGHT: All over the country beautiful decorative ironwork was requisitioned to provide iron to make war weapons. Much of it was unsuitable and left lying in unsightly heaps as Mrs Hazel Macnaughten tells her son in a letter to him in 1941. 'I am writing to the Town Clerk, making a protest against our lovely iron gate etc., being seized I hear they may seize them at any time now. They don't even bother to gather up the metal and other stuff all over the country, which is lying in heaps, defacing the scenery. It is to make a kind of gesture at the public expense, as usual.'

In this picture of a wartime wedding the bride has found herself a white wedding dress. The skirt, separate from the blouse top, is made from parachute silk which was a beautiful material which did not require clothing coupons. Defective parachutes were sold very cheaply to the civilian population and used for making various garments including wedding dresses.

Important Official Notice.

BOROUGH OF NEW WINDSOR.

EMERGENCY POWERS (DEFENCE) ACTS, 1939 AND 1940.

REQUISITION OF UNNECESSARY IRON RAILINGS, ETC.

Acting under a Direction of the Minister of Supply, the Town Council proposes to schedule the iron railings, gates, posts, chains, bollards and similar articles on this property as unnecessary and available for removal.

An appeal against the inclusion of these railings, etc., in the schedule may be lodged on the following grounds only :—

(i) that the Railings, etc., should be maintained for safety reasons ;

(ii) that the Railings, etc., are necessary to prevent cattle, etc., from straying ;

(iii) that the Railings, etc., are of special artistic merit or of historic interest ;

(iv) that the Railings, etc., serve a useful function and, if removed, would require replacement by some other form of material.

If you wish to lodge such appeal it must be sent in writing within fourteen days to the Borough Engineer, 16, Alma Road, Windsor, and must give the following information :—

(a) full details of the railings, etc. ;

(b) their exact situation ;

(c) the category (i), (ii), (iii) or (iv) above under which exclusion is claimed.

It is hoped that owners will be prepared to make a free gift of their railings, etc., to the nation, but property owners and others whose interests are affected by the removal will be given the opportunity of claiming compensation at the time the removal takes place. Details will be advertised in the local newspaper when the time comes.

J. W. HAMBIDGE,
Town Clerk.

14, PARK STREET,
        WINDSOR.
October, 1941.

If the Occupier is not the Owner of the premises, he is asked to send this Notice to the Owner immediately.

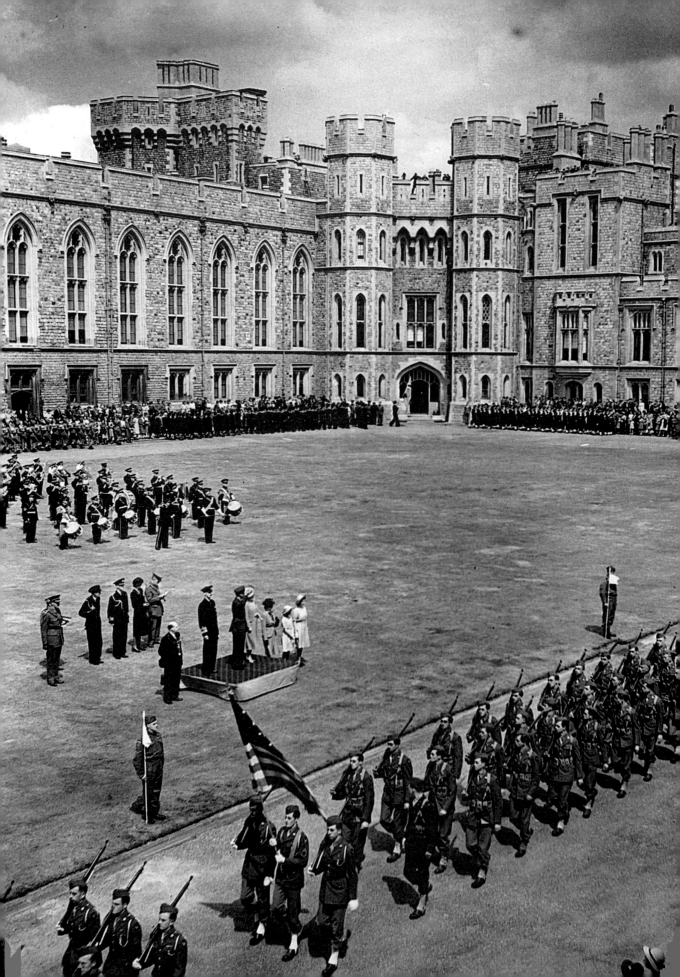

Windsor's beauty contest was won by Thelma Kirtland whose brother dared her £5 that she wouldn't enter the competition; 'So I did,' said Thelma. Her prize was £10 and a course of riding lessons at the local stables. Her dress was made by her mother and is typical of the 1940s with its padded shoulders, sweetheart neckline and threequarter-length sleeves. There was a great deal more home dressmaking during the war years as ready-made clothes took more clothing coupons. Her curly hair was achieved by the use of wartime setting lotion (cold tea and sugar water) and sleeping in her Dinky curlers.

PREVIOUS PAGE: The first American GI soldiers were seen in Windsor in 1943. As D-Day approached their numbers increased. They had bases in Holyport and near Ascot and regarded Windsor as a place of recreation where they would attend the dances. The Americans were popular with the local children and the young women as they were generous with gifts of chewing gum and nylons.

At the end of the war the lights went on again and this picture is taken from the Guildhall.

The ending of the war in
May 1945 was celebrated
all over the land with
street parties. This one is
for the children of Arthur
Road. The women have
come straight from their
houses and are dressed
informally in their
'pinnies' as is Mrs
Chatworthy one of the
organisers in the
foreground. Joe Brooks,
one of the other
organisers was the local
ARP warden.

Post-war Windsor and Eton: Merger with Maidenhead and Expansion of the Town

THE second half of the 20th century saw the country still reeling from the effects of World War Two. The resources of the once rich country were spent and the population continued to endure even worse rationing and austerity. While other towns were trying to recover from the devastation of the war, Windsor and Eton had an added burden; the River Thames had flooded again and the towns were cleaning themselves up.

Following weeks of terrible weather, the greatest flood of the century paralysed the Thames Valley leaving thousands homeless and a huge area facing the worst natural catastrophe in living memory. Along the course of the river the towns of Windsor, Eton and Maidenhead, plus their adjoining villages, were inundated and inhabitants were forced to evacuate their homes. Many remained but moved to upstairs rooms. Some areas were completely dislocated. By 19 March 1947 the river was a mile and a half wide, the flood extending from Vansittart Road in the south to the Electric Light Works at Slough in the north.

In the previous month there had been a fuel crisis which had followed the long cruel winter. Supplies of all fuels were in such short supply that the street lights were dimmed and electricity was rationed. There were reports of the elderly dying in their freezing homes.

The mood in Windsor during the 1950s was much as the rest of the country. Rationing was still in force and much of the euphoria which had followed the ending of the war had worn off and people were impatient that shortages were still present. This had shown itself when Princess Elizabeth married Prince Philip in 1947. Her beautiful wedding dress caused much sour comment. Why should the princess have a lovely dress while the rest of the people had to put up with clothes rationing? Despite this discontent the popularity of the King and Queen was as great as ever, a fact graphically illustrated when King George VI died suddenly in February 1952. As the Sebastopol Bell in the Round Tower tolled 56 times for the years of the king's life, the people were stunned by his death.

The funeral took place in Windsor on 15 February and the town was closed from 10am. People lined the route to watch the gun carriage which bore the coffin of the king pass through the town from Windsor and Eton station, where it had arrived from Westminster. Naval personnel from HMS *Vanguard* had the privilege of pulling the gun carriage, a privilege which dated from the funeral of Queen Victoria. Following the gun carriage were 30 members of the foreign royal families who walked three abreast, and who were followed by heads of foreign

The 1947 floods were the worst in the Thames Valley in living memory.

Special Missions and the High Commissioners. There was a guard of honour of Grenadier Guards plus the RAF and the route was lined by soldiers from six regiments and the cadets from five schools. At 2pm the coffin was taken into St George's Chapel and, as it entered, there was a two-minute silence throughout the town.

After the funeral, we see the first signs of the tourist invasion which would influence the development of the town for the rest of the century.

There were 180,000 visitors over the weekend which followed the funeral of the king. Many people said that they 'wanted to make a pilgrimage to the resting place of King George VI'. Another factor which would eventually contribute to the increase in tourists was that the new Queen would spend much more time in the royal town.

Almost immediately into her reign the Queen started to stay at Windsor for Easter, for the Garter ceremony and for the Ascot races.

As the second half of the century proceeded more leisure time became available and young people were able to spend that time on sport as recreation land was donated to sports clubs. In the mid-1950s television started to take over from the cinema as the main leisure activity. But there was still a choice of four cinemas for the residents of Windsor and Eton, and even the theatre also served as a cinema for a period.

Practically the entire population watched television coverage of the Coronation, which was the event of the decade. The Coronation of Elizabeth II took place on 2 June 1953 and nearly everyone who could was watching the television transmission of the ceremony which was taking place in Westminster Abbey. Many people did not have a TV set of their own and instead crowded into the homes of friends and neighbours to watch the programme.

Saturday 13 June 1953, was Windsor and Eton's great day when the newly-crowned monarch would make a state entry into Windsor via Eton. In the previous week, there were many parties for children and the elderly, balls and banquets, carnival processions, exhibitions and open air dances. All the shops and businesses were decorated in blue and gold and stands were erected around the walls of the castle. The townspeople were able to buy a place to view the state entry for 5s to sit on the grass or £3 3s 0d for the best view. The *Windsor Express* estimated that 100,000 people watched the Queen's procession from Slough through Eton up into the town of Windsor until it reached the Park Street entrance to the Long Walk, where a sea of schoolchildren shouted themselves hoarse.

The people of Windsor and Eton had waited along the entire route for over six hours for a sight of the Queen.

In the following years of the decade there were plans for a public footpath along the Thames from Teddington to Cricklade – a distance of 136 miles. Many of the public had never seen the full beauty of the river as access was limited due to the bank's use as a towpath for the barges which transported goods. The barge trade had declined as goods were transported on the railways and roads.

By the 1960s the town was in need of a facelift. On 12 May 1961 the Queen and Prince Philip, along with the mayors of some 500 cities and towns, celebrated the completion of a Civic Trust project which included the re-decoration of the shops and houses and the removal of ugly street furniture.

New buildings began to transform the historic face of the ancient town of Windsor in the 1970s. One of the ugliest and most controversial was the Ward Royal which was completed just before the 1970s building boom. It won prizes from the Ministry of Housing and Local Government but this did not endear it to the people of the town although the building comprises pleasant flats for the occupants. Its monolithic fortress-like appearance, even in this new century, still presents a soulless disfigurement of a charming town.

New developments to the west of Windsor saw the construction of council housing estates including high-rise flats as in Sawyers Close. The word 'high-rise' is hardly appropriate when we consider the scale of these modest structures in comparison with the soaring tower blocks in other parts of the country.

The needs of the expanding population in relation to churches were met by the building of three new churches in the Dedworth area. These include St Mark's Catholic Church and All Saints' Anglican Church, both in Dedworth Road, and the Baptist Church in Smith's Lane. New schools were also built in this period.

How a town deals with the problem of cars is one of the biggest challenges which a local authority has to meet. In a tourist town such as Windsor, where the tide of visitors has now risen to 4,000,000 a year, there are no easy solutions. King Edward Court is a pleasing combination of car parking and retail centre. Opened by the Queen in March 1980 it was built as a shopping area with spaces for 940 cars. However, by the end of the century Windsor is again at saturation point and the council is seeking more spaces for yet more cars.

The expansion of Heathrow airport is a constant problem to those who live under the flight path which includes the residents of Windsor and Eton. Many people work at Heathrow but the residents of the town are made miserable by the constant air traffic.

In the last decade of the millennium a fire at the castle on 20 November 1992 focussed world attention on Windsor. It was caused by a spotlight igniting a curtain in the Queen's private chapel during a major refurbishment of the castle. As TV images flashed round the world so the press rushed to Windsor to record a spectacular event. The fire came at the end of what the Queen called her 'annus horribilis'. But five years later the castle reopened the restored state apartments to unanimous admiration. If the fire had been a disaster, the restoration was a triumph and even more tourists flocked into Windsor to see its greatest attraction.

Some tourist attractions closed but others replaced them, such as the Safari Park which closed after 25 years and which was replaced by Legoland, run by the Danish toy company, Lego. The 1990s was a decade of closures. The nuns at the Community of St John the Baptist at Clewer decided to leave their convent after 148 years of devoted work in education, nursing and social work and relocate to Oxford while their work continues in India.

The Royal Free School closed, thus ending its 178 years of history. The Magistrates Court closed after 560 years of justice being dispensed locally. The hospital at Old Windsor closed and was turned into housing. The exhibition of Royalty and Empire closed and became a shopping precinct.

As the year ended on 31 December 1999, the people of Windsor and Eton were as conscious as any that the next day would herald a new century.

In 1947 the river was 1½ miles wide by 19 March and the flood extended from Vansittart Road in the south to the Electric Light Works at Slough in the north.

Cleaning up in Grosvenor Place after the 1947 flood waters have receded.

Children had no dry areas in which to play and the floods had reduced the recreation grounds to swamps.

Once the 1947 floods receded the cleaning up process had to begin, assisted by the army.

Eton was also inundated and these Eton schoolboys, without their wellington boots, seem reluctant to step into the flood water.

The Great Freeze in the winter of 1962–3.

The Post Office at the junction of Park Street and High Street which has now been demolished to make way for yet another office block.

Oxford Road was demolished to make way for Ward Royal. The road contained small shops such as a fishmonger, bakery, a corn and seed merchant and a confectionery and tobacconist shop. Such businesses were already under threat both from the arrival of the supermarkets and the departure of their customers to live elsewhere. The sign on the right is for the Why Not? public house.

This controversial building, which was completed in 1969, caused a great deal of comment, not all of it positive. It won prizes from the Ministry of Housing and Local Government but it failed to convince the residents of the borough that it was the right type of building for an historic town. Although the individual flats are pleasant places in which to live, the overall effect of the building in such a position, is an obtrusive one.

Sawyers Close, Dedworth. This block of council flats, although classified as 'high rise' does not disfigure the area and are a pleasing addition to the domestic architecture of the town.

12 May 1961. A Civic Trust project which co-ordinated the redecoration of the shops and houses in the town, removing unsightly street signs and ugly street lamps, was completed. The Queen, accompanied by the Duke of Edinburgh, visited the town along with the mayors of other towns and cities to celebrate the Windsor Facelift.

The town council is gathered outside the door of the parish church following the civic service which is an annual event. This particular service was held on 31 March 1973 and marked the last day of the existence of the Royal Borough of New Windsor. On 1 April 1973, the Borough of Maidenhead, Cookham Rural District Council and Eton Rural District Council were incorporated into the Royal Borough of Windsor and Maidenhead.

In the front row is David Drye, the deputy mayor and his wife; the MP for Windsor, Dr Alan Glyn and Lady Glyn. In front is the mayoress, Mrs Gwen Procter, then the town clerk, George Waldram and his wife; the mayor, John Procter; the honorary recorder, Frank Blennerhassett, and the mayor's chaplain. The macebearer is Harry Bates. Nine of the 10 aldermen are present, wearing their fur-trimmed robes, and the others are either councillors – 30 of the 40 are present – or officers of the council.

Baronness Flather of Windsor and Maidenhead was the first Asian woman mayor in the country when she became the mayor of Windsor and Maidenhead in 1986–7.

View over the rooftops. In the middle of the picture is the roof of the King Edward car park that blends successfully with the rest of the architecture in Windsor.

The traditional market, a descendant of the original mediaeval market, was set up on Bachelors' Acre until recently.

Children playing in the fountains of Bachelors' Acre. Windsor resident, Doris Mellor, fought a long hard fight to keep this area as an open space when the council wanted to turn it into a car park. Her efforts were rewarded in 1975, when the House of Lords decided that Bachelors' Acre was subject to a customary right of the inhabitants to indulge in lawful sports and pastimes.

The station, which was the terminus for the Great Western Railway's route between Paddington and Windsor, was opened in October 1849 and used by Queen Victoria and her court as early as November 1849. A new station was built to celebrate the Queen's Diamond Jubilee in 1897 but was not finished in time for that event. Madame Tussaud's bought the station in 1979 and put on the Royalty and Empire exhibition which later closed and became the present Windsor Royal Station shopping complex. The trains which use this station now run only between Slough and Windsor.

The tourists are gathering outside The Harte and Garter Hotel, ready for their guide to lead them round Windsor Castle. The White Hart was one of the many taverns which played an important role in the life of Tudor England. As it was opposite the castle, it was much favoured by peers and knights. The Garter, which was nearby, was preferred by country gentlemen and those of lesser rank. Windsor had a substantial number of such taverns, inns and alehouses and their landlords were usually men of influence in the town. The two historic inns now form one modern hotel catering especially for coach parties of tourists.

This modern view from Windsor and Eton Bridge shows the effect of pedestrianisation. No vehicles have been able to pass over the bridge since June 1975.

On Friday 20 November 1992 fire swept through Windsor Castle, partially destroying the north-east wing and devastating six magnificent rooms, including St George's Hall, the Queen's private chapel and four reception rooms. Three towers were also badly damaged: Brunswick Tower, Chester Tower and the Prince of Wales' Tower. Fortunately, the contents of the castle, considered one of the world's greatest collection of art treasures, were saved and only a few items were lost or damaged.

St George's Hall in January 1993. The first process of clearing away the debris has begun and the badly damaged timbers can be seen lying on the floor. Some timbers are still in place above the minstrel gallery. The floor and walls suffered mainly smoke and water damage.

When the Waterloo Chamber was reopened to the public after the fire, visitors were intrigued to see the paintings of pantomime fairytale characters which filled the gilded picture frames. A talented 15-year-old artist, called Charles Whatham, who was evacuated to Windsor during the war, painted these in 1944. The oil paintings by Sir Thomas Lawrence which usually adorned the Waterloo Chamber had been removed for safekeeping for the duration of the war. In their place, these posters were an inspirational adornment to the room while the performance of *Old Mother Red Riding Boots* was taking place, and King George VI decreed that the posters should remain even when the oil paintings were eventually replaced.

By the beginning of 1993, a temporary roof covered the exposed structure of St George's Hall, while the initial assessment of the damage and plans for restoration were considered.

Thames Valley Athletics Centre, Eton. The centre opened in May 1999 as a Community Athletics Centre after the Royal Borough of Windsor and Maidenhead, Slough Borough Council and Eton College formed a partnership to apply for a grant from the National Lottery Sports Fund. It has an eight-lane all-weather running track and a stadium for 600 spectators, plus facilities for indoor training and a fully equipped gym.

The Sisters of the Community of St John the Baptist at Clewer have left their convent after 148 years in the area. Here two of the nuns are checking their records.

MILLENNIUM WINDSOR AND ETON:
INTERNATIONALLY FAMOUS TOURIST TOWN AND COLLEGE

THE new millennium opened with a bang. On 31 December 1999 some 3,000 visitors to Legoland counted down the seconds to midnight and as Big Ben chimed the last second, transmitted from London, the sky exploded with the noise and flash of fireworks. As we move into the 21st century it is an appropriate time to compare modern Windsor with its past.

Some things never change. The river remains, although now as a source of pleasure and leisure with its pretty gardens and tranquil banks, rather than the trading artery of its past. Perhaps the Flood Alleviation Scheme will tame the river at last, for in each century the River Thames has shown the inhabitants of Windsor and Eton its destructive power.

The town continues to flourish watched over by the majestic castle which draws to it an increasing number of tourists. International companies seek to place their offices in Windsor, a town with a castle that is known all over the world.

The castle, too, remains, its magnificent outline against the sky, its state rooms beautifully restored after the great fire of 1992. The monarch continues to reside in Windsor, a place she regards as her home, with Buckingham Palace as her office. Her soldiers still provide the pageantry with their daily guard mounting and annual Garter ceremony. These soldiers are no mere 'chocolate box' decoration for in the later years of the 20th century, they fought in the Falklands and Gulf wars and fulfilled a peacekeeping role in Bosnia.

However, the people have changed. In our mobile society, with its shifting population, the residents of Windsor and Eton now come from all over the world to settle here, some for a short period others for longer. The original settlers of Anglo-Saxons and Celts dislodged so decisively by the Normans at the beginning of this history have been joined by many other nationalities.

The town came into being to supply services to the castle and its garrison. The small market expanded into shops and the taverns evolved into hotels. History has turned full circle with the castle shop now serving the town.

In 2001, the Royal Farm Shop opened its doors to the townsfolk and serves them a variety of products including fine game, beef, lamb and poultry, organically grown vegetables, dairy products from the royal dairy and Old Windsor Dark Ale brewed exclusively by Old Luxters Farm Brewery, Hambledon, near Henley, Oxon.

One of Windsor's newest buildings is the handsome office block, Windsor Dials, which houses the international company, FM Global and Galileo House, a travel company.

The site of the latest office block on Maidenhead Road has 12,850 square metres and is a sign of the changing face of Windsor. International companies like to have an address in Royal Windsor as the town is known throughout the world. The proximity of London and the international airport of Heathrow also make Windsor an attractive base.

Nell Gwynn is thought to have lived in Church Street at one time. She was the most famous of Charles II's many mistresses. Our 'pretty, witty Nell' would no doubt have had something saucy to say about the present use of Nell Gwynn House as an internet café.

The ancient ceremony of swan upping, which usually takes place in the month of July, is to mark all the new cygnets with the same mark as their parents. The mute swan is a much-prized bird and was given royal status in the 12th century. To own swans was a status symbol, so they are marked to show to whom they belong. Swans 'flying free' belong to the sovereign and are not marked. The picture shows a small flotilla of skiffs which arrived at Romney Lock in the afternoon of 17 July 2001. The crews, who will be carrying out the swan upping, started their journey at Sunbury. Two skiffs carry the Queen's Standard and the other four skiffs carry the flags of the companies of the Vintners or the Dyers. While the level of water rises in the lock the crew stand up in their boats (rather precariously) and toast the Queen.

Mute swans are Britain's only resident species of swans and gather in large groups along the length of the Thames. They are joined by moorhens, coots and the mallard duck.

Although Windsor has been somewhat urbanised, there are still many tranquil places by the river. This part of the Thames once serviced Clewer Mill.

Plans for the Flood Alleviation Scheme began soon after the severe floods of 1947. Work did not begin on the huge engineering project until 1996. Costing £100 million, it was given the name Jubilee River and was first used in February 2002. In the picture members of the local club of Soroptimist International are being given a guided tour of the work in progress in the summer of 2001 when the project was nearly finished.

The Royal Farm Shop was opened to the public in 2001 and sells produce from the royal estates.

A sad postscript. The funeral cortège of the Queen Mother arrives at Windsor on 9 April 2002.